The Dewey Color System®

The Dewey Color System®

CHOOSE YOUR COLORS, CHANGE YOUR LIFE

DEWEY SADKA

THREE RIVERS PRESS • NEW YORK

Published by Three Rivers Press, New York, New York.
Member of the Crown Publishing Group,
a division of Random House, Inc.
www.crownpublishing.com

Originally published in slightly different form by Energia®, Inc.,
in 2001. Copyright © 2001 by Energia®, Inc.

THREE RIVERS PRESS and the Tugboat design are registered
trademarks of Random House, Inc.

Printed in the United States of America

Design by Robert Bull

Library of Congress Cataloging-in-Publication Data

Sadka, Dewey.
The Dewey color system : choose your colors, change your life /
Dewey Sadka.—1st ed.
1. Color—Psychological aspects.   2. Personality tests.
3. Self-evaluation.   I. Title.
BF789.C7 S23 2004
155.2'84—dc22   2003018421

ISBN 1-4000-5062-6

10   9   8   7   6   5   4   3   2   1

First Revised Edition

CONTENTS

Part Three

Learning Your Self-Truth to
Uncomplicate Your Life

Part Four

Making Each Moment a
Celebration of You

The Dewey Color System®

WHY I CREATED THE DEWEY COLOR SYSTEM®

Refining the talents of others has been my life's work. For more than eighteen years, as the director and owner of one of the nation's largest employee-staffing companies, I found it especially rewarding to look beyond the surface, to try to see the inner workings of each person.

By constantly encouraging my employees and clients to express their heartfelt thoughts, I became aware of their feelings and needs. This allowed me to identify the things that motivated them. My efforts to make each of them a winner made me a winner. In less than eighteen years, I turned the $30,000 investment I used to start my business into a $38 million company.

Since I believe that people achieve success when they do what they enjoy, I began searching for a simple key to better understand the desires, concerns, different perspectives, and passions of those individuals who would determine my future.

My experiences with traditional personality evaluations, such as the well-known Myers-Briggs testing tool, led me to conclude that they only scratched the surface of understanding an individual. I knew that if I could invent an evaluation that revealed the motivating factors of each person, productivity, sales, and employee morale would surely soar.

Working in the staffing-services business for more than twenty-four years, I learned how thousands of people react during periods of crisis. After many years of observing others, I found that often I could predict people's actions and the eventual outcome of particular situations. This inspired me to look for patterns of human behavior that would tend to repeat themselves. My goal was to gain a more objective view of the needs of others and myself.

THE CONCEPT

Chemistry and biology have physical structures that give them predictability. Biologists, for example, can analyze a blood cell and detect patterns that will tend to repeat under certain conditions. So why not seek to identify those patterns in human behavior as well?

The Dewey Color System® is based on the concept that color can be used to reveal the core of an individual's personality. Concept-based theories have given the world its most far-reaching inventions. Here are a few:

- "The earth is not the center of the universe"
  —Copernicus
- "Time stands still at the speed of light"—Albert Einstein
- "A machine can think"—Alan Turing

The Dewey Color System allows you to learn about yourself without feeling the pain of personally invasive questions or stumbling through trying to find the right words to answer them. Don't let the fact that it's so easy discount the truth of this new system.

I've broken *The Dewey Color System* into four parts. In Part One you'll learn how to use this system, which explains *you* in compelling detail and with astounding accuracy. In Part Two, you'll discover what makes you passionate, how you react to situations, what gets you excited in love, and what makes you successful in your career. In Part Three, you'll read about how you can uncomplicate your life by understanding what drives you and slows you down as a human being. And in Part Four, you'll learn how to make your world work for you by participating in some revealing exercises, assessing your self-test results, and learning invaluable tips for keeping your priorities strong.

MY MISSION

I've spent twenty-eight years developing and refining this system, and my greatest wish is that this proven, reliable method of using color to map your inner self will give you the knowledge to create positive changes in your life without compromising the passionate strength within you.

Part One

Discovering the
Dewey Color System

CHAPTER ONE

Discovering Your True Colors

This above all, to thine own self be true.
—WILLIAM SHAKESPEARE

Genuine love, personal happiness, and professional success begin and continue to grow when you know what you want from life. It's simply not enough, however, to say, "I want this." You need to understand *why* you want it.

It all starts with you being yourself. When you know who you are, determining what you want is a breeze. Yet we constantly deceive ourselves in order to fit in or to make things work.

The Dewey Color System will bring you back home to *you.* Language-based tests define behavior; color preference evokes your personality, that part of you that never changes. You'll read about what's most fun for you and why you love to do it. What's fascinating is that you'll be more successful as you realize that what you do best just happens to be what you enjoy most.

Self-truth is always the simplest and best path. As you read through the meanings of your color selections, reconnect with the child you once were, the colorful youngster who had no fears or inhibitions. As you focus on your true self, you'll gradually quit avoiding the parts of your personality you often try to suppress for whatever reason, be it social convention or simply the pressures of modern life. Your true self—your own personal greatness that is the *real* you—will ultimately be revealed!

HOW THE SYSTEM CONFIRMS YOUR LIFE'S FOCUS

By focusing on your preferences for precise shades of color, the Dewey Color System indicates who you are and how you relate to others as well as how you make decisions, solve problems, and approach the world. Because this analysis enhances your self-knowledge, you'll gain the confidence to determine what you want, and the focus to help you get it.

The system uses the subliminal power of color to reveal your core being—the basis for why you do what you do. Using only color preference, it bypasses language to reveal what's most important in your life. The Dewey Color System establishes how we prioritize our basic needs and goals. Color preference is innate. A preferred color, for example, visually inspires people to feel their hopes and aspirations. A nonpreferred color irritatingly reminds them of what is missing in their life.

CHANGE YOUR LIFE, NOT YOURSELF

In our fast-paced world, we are bombarded with situations in which we have to make decisions that determine our tomorrow. Knowing exactly what you most enjoy will keep you on track and give you the self-confidence to make each day fun. Life is not about being someone; it's about being yourself.

Passionate, focused energy is very contagious. All of a sudden, you'll find yourself speaking from your heart, surrounded by positive support, and proud of your contributions. In reading *The Dewey Color System*, you'll better understand what you can expect not only from situations or other people, but from yourself.

WHO ARE YOUR FRIENDS AND LOVED ONES?

Discovering your friends' and loved ones' talents will help you understand why these people are so important in your life. When you comprehend their passions and fears, you'll gain the patience and understanding to give them enthusiastic support. Read *The Dewey Color System* with the people you're close to. You'll have meaningful conversations that strengthen your relationships with them.

Children are great with colors. Not nearly as bewildered by choice as adults, they select their colors quickly and with remarkable self-assurance. If you have young children over three years old, translate the meaning of their color choices for them. The tremendous personal insights they'll gain will help them to develop a strong sense of self-esteem. And by understanding their passions, you'll gain the power to better support them without destroying their essence.

FIVE EASY STEPS TO SELF-TRUTH:
HOW TO USE THE DEWEY COLOR SYSTEM®

Step #1: Pick Your Colors

First, turn to the color blocks following page 24 and select your favorite and least favorite color within the primary, secondary, achromatic, and intermediate categories. Write them down on "My Color Category Page" for easy reference (see page 13).

Step #2: Determine Your Energy Type
Combine Your Primary and Secondary Colors to See Yourself; Add Your Achromatic Color to Reveal How Others See You

Then combine your favorite primary and secondary selections and, in your personalized color chapter, read about how you see yourself. (For instance, if your favorite primary and secondary choices are red and purple, turn to Chapter 11 to read your general profile.) Here is a listing of all the primary and secondary combinations and their personalized color chapters:

Chapter 4   "Yellow and Green: The Caretakers"

Chapter 5   "Yellow and Purple: The Catalysts"

Chapter 6   "Yellow and Orange: The Technical Thinkers"

Chapter 7   "Blue and Green: The Anchors"

Chapter 8   "Blue and Purple: The Thinkers"

Chapter 9   "Blue and Orange: The Builders"

Next, add your favorite achromatic (black, white, or brown) selection to understand how others see you.

(For example, if you are a red-purple and add white as your achromatic selection, after you read about how you see yourself, turn to the red-purple-white profile later in your personalized color chapter.)

Note: You can turn to the color blocks following page 24 and pick your colors right now, or read through the rest of Part One if you'd like to gain more background on the Dewey Color System before you begin your journey.

Step #3: Dig Deep to Evoke Your Desires

In Chapters 13–15 your favorite and least-favorite color selections in the three categories reveal the upside and downside of your passions and fears. Read about them in detail.

Step #4: Look at Your Intermediate Colors

Now explore the fourth color category and read about your intermediate selections to see how you make your world work for you. (See Chapter 16, "Taking On the World.")

Step #5: Celebrate Yourself

Read Chapter 17, "Change Your Life, Not Yourself." Use the color summaries, stories, and in-depth exercises to experience how to redirect your thoughts and behaviors without compromising the passionate power within you.

PICK YOUR COLORS

You are about to begin a quest that will deepen your understanding of yourself and intensify your passion for life. Be prepared to view a new, yet somehow familiar, perspective of who you are, what you do, and why you do it.

GET READY!

- There are no right or wrong choices—only your choices.
- Your choices aren't about what "looks good" on you or your sofa. They're about what you're naturally attracted to, what makes you feel good.
- Don't rush. Feel the colors. Let them pick you!

Turn to the color blocks following page 24 to make your color selections.

MY COLOR CATEGORY PAGE

Your color category selections:

CATEGORY	FAVORITE	LEAST FAVORITE
Primary		
Secondary		
Achromatic		
Intermediate		

CHAPTER TWO

The Dewey Color System®

Imagine a system so understandable and so much fun that even a child could use it. It would be nothing short of revolutionary. Well, here you have it.

So, what is the science behind color, and why are we attracted to or repelled by particular colors? Color is a reflection of light. This reflection is what you see. It is received through the pupil of your eye in the form of varying wavelengths. This energy has a physical quality that each person reacts to differently.

Even though nothing inherently has a color, its reflection is interpreted by your brain as a distinguishable quality. Its vibration creates an unspoken energy. Yellow, for example, is widely considered to be irritating. But if you are a person who prefers yellow, you will find it inspirational.

This is the first evaluation system to extensively use color preference to bypass language. Instead of relying on lengthy, imprecise questionnaires, the Dewey Color System uses a simple, highly accurate methodology based on your color preferences to reveal who you are—not who you believe yourself to be.

The Dewey Color System has received a patent for its ability to recognize the connection between personality and the four distinct color categories: primary colors, secondary colors, achromatic colors, and intermediate colors. It incorporates employee-evaluation systems, once available only to the professional community, and turns them into a valuable new test accessible to the public. After reading *The Dewey Color System,* you will find hundreds of uses for it in your everyday life.

A RELIABLE SYSTEM

There are two ways we access knowledge—via concepts and experimentation. With the help of leading academic scholars, I put my concept to a rigorous test with well over five thousand color profiles that took eight years to develop.

In clinical comparison of my system with America's leading personality-evaluation systems—the Myers-Briggs, the 16PF, and the Strong Interest Inventory—the following results were indicated:

- Two out of three participants believed that the Dewey Color System gave them a stronger awareness of themselves.
- Three out of four participants believed that the Dewey Color System better described how they live their lives.

A BRIEF HISTORICAL PERSPECTIVE

Since the beginning of civilization, we human beings have labored to discover the hidden motivations behind our actions. This effort has led to an abundance of systems that hold one thing in common: the endeavor to categorize and uncover our real selves.

Early attempts to create a system of self-discovery led the curious to focus on external influences such as the stars, fate, or the elements. This gave rise to numerous systems that are still popular today.

Modern times, however, found investigators looking at the individual and free will. Gradually, empirical observation replaced even the most detailed systems of folklore and witchcraft, and in turn paved the way for psychology and the analysis of human behavior.

However, one thing has stymied all of these systems and those who administer them—the imprecision of language. Why? Simple. What happens, for example, if questions aren't asked properly? What if the people being questioned interpret them differently? What role does stress, fatigue, environment, prejudice, bias, and education play in the skewing of test results? Also, people frequently deceive themselves and fail to answer questions with complete honesty.

For all these reasons, experts have longed to create a language-free system to tell us about individual identity.

COLOR IS NOW A LANGUAGE

The solution to the problems of language-based tests was as simple as it was elegant. Color! How could anything be more obvious? Why not use color as an indicator of personality? No longer would there be a need to rely on words. Color could allow you to ask questions without words. The confusion of meanings and interpretation would be altogether eliminated.

Nature Knows Best

The Dewey Color System came from observing nature. Originally, I examined the apparent functions of each color in nature in order to describe it in language—to give each hue a verbal meaning. For example, green exists only where there is fertile soil. Isn't this the essence of nurturing?

Visit deweycolorsystem.com to learn more about how the system evolved. Also check out the language evolution of each color at the end of Chapters 13, 14, 15, and 16 to better understand your essence.

Your Personality Is a Combination of Colors

As you read, keep in mind that each color category is a layer that acts autonomously, as if the others don't exist. Primary colors are your basic motivators, the fuel in your engine. Secondaries show how you relate to others and process your thoughts about them. Achromatics explain your core being, your hopes and fears. Intermediates expose how you take on the world.

As you explore your color preferences, keep in mind that your personality reflects a combination of colors, not just a single color.

Color Unlocks Your Most Intimate Thoughts

Each color represents a personal value you need to honor. Your color selection reveals the rewards and consequences of how you prioritize in your life.

Use the color interpretations in the system to embrace the passions within yourself, to respect the motivations of those you love, and to electrify your life. You will gain the courage and confidence to do what you do best.

Celebrate Yourself

Here's your chance to be affirmed for your greatness. Stress, constantly striving to make money, or being consumed by what needs to be done can distract you from celebrating yourself. Personal growth begins with accepting yourself just as you are right now. As you read, celebrate your unique talents and the power within you by reviewing the contributions and gifts you have given to others.

Knowing who you really are and what you want will better equip you to handle and solve life's problems. You'll have a better understanding of how to have more passion in your life, relationships, and career.

FREQUENTLY ASKED QUESTIONS

Can I Make a Mistake?

It's unlikely that you'll choose a color that's not meant for you. How can you not choose what you already instinctively know? However, if the personality descriptions based on the colors you initially choose seem to be off the mark, read about the other colors and see which apply the most to you. Then, choose your colors again. Could it be that you are avoiding your basic self?

If you have a strong reaction to the color description, good or bad, you've probably picked the right color. You'll tend to feel indifference when reading about your incorrect colors. If you're someone who works with colors a lot, such as a painter or graphic designer, it can be especially difficult to make your selection.

If you feel that your colors do not reflect who you are now, they might be showing your core-personality responses, not your actions. Training and experience have taught you lessons that allow you to change the way you act. Get upset, though, and you'll need to struggle to keep the core part of you from taking over.

What If I'm Color-Blind?

The system is still functional. It will just take you longer to make your choices. So, take your time. Generally, you will dislike the colors you cannot see. You will have an emotional need to learn and express what these color areas represent.

Will My Colors Change?

You bet! When your life changes, so can your colors. Leaving home, getting married, having children, losing someone close to you—all of these events can change your color preferences. For the most part, however, your colors change in varying degrees and not as dramatically as you might think.

If your color choices change, read about your new colors in the color-change paragraphs at the end of Chapters 13, 14, 15, and 16. You will gain insight into your current needs.

In the Dewey Color System, to ensure accuracy, we used the spectrum's most brilliant colors. Studies have proven the more vibrant the color, the more distinct the response.

What If I Like All the Colors?

If you are someone who loves color, selecting a preferred color can be difficult. Artists, designers, and those who work with color every day can even have trouble picking their least favorite colors. If you are someone that has everyday contact with color, you might have to go back and pick again. The second time, eliminate your thoughts about how you use color—make it all about you.

What If I Can't Choose between Two Colors?

Go ahead. Dig deep and pick one. Later, read the meaning of both colors. One color probably represents who you are and the other one is probably who you feel you need to be. Are you going through a transitional period?

HOW MANY OF ME ARE THERE?

The listing below represents a ranking of color choices from a sample population of approximately four thousand people. Once you've made your primary, secondary, and intermediate color choices, view where you fall from among these twenty-seven energy types. The higher you rank, the more you are understood.

1. Blue-Green-White	10. Blue-Purple-Brown	19. Red-Purple-Brown
2. Blue-Purple-Black	11. Yellow-Green-White	20. Yellow-Purple-Brown
3. Blue-Green-Black	12. Yellow-Purple-Black	21. Blue-Orange-White
4. Blue-Green-Brown	13. Red-Green-Brown	22. Yellow-Green-Brown
5. Red-Purple-Black	14. Red-Purple-White	23. Yellow-Orange-Black
6. Blue-Purple-White	15. Yellow-Green-Black	24. Blue-Orange-Brown
7. Red-Green-Black	16. Yellow-Orange-White	25. Yellow-Orange-Brown
8. Red-Green-White	17. Red-Orange-Black	26. Red-Orange-Brown
9. Yellow-Purple-White	18. Blue-Orange-Black	27. Red-Orange-White

CHAPTER THREE

Choose Your Colors, Change Your Life

Each of the color categories represents different aspects of your personality: motivation, hidden agendas, fears, temperament, perception, coping mechanisms, interpersonal skills, strengths, weaknesses, hopes, and ambitions.

Your favorite colors represent your hopes and aspirations, the ideals you pursue with passion. The more you accept this passionate part of yourself, the more successful you will be. These colors also reveal the difficulties you experience when you make your passions your only priority.

Your least favorite colors are as significant as your favorites. They highlight the issues and experiences that you try to avoid facing. Dealing with what you would normally avoid is essential to your personal growth. It allows you to better manage your life.

Your favorite and least favorite selections will reveal the twin forces in your life. In gaining a greater awareness of your personality, passions, and power, you'll acquire the knowledge to create positive change without destroying your essence.

USE #1: GET TO KNOW YOURSELF

Too many of us wander through life with uncertainty and a lack of clarity. It's the unknown, the incomprehensible that leads to fear, resentment, loneliness, failure, and even poverty. Once you understand yourself, everything begins to flow: love, wisdom, strength, happiness, and serenity.

Your life today is richer because color was used to indicate chemical reactions in science and medicine. The Dewey Color System takes you beyond these established uses of color to shed light on how you approach nearly every aspect of your life.

USE #2: LEARN ABOUT FRIENDS AND LOVED ONES

Reading the Dewey Color System with those closest to you will allow you to see what is special about you and your relationships. When you comprehend your friends' and loved ones' fears, you will have more patience to help them in times of crisis. We have provided space at the back of the book for you to record the colors of friends and loved ones. (See "Additional Color Pages," pages 235–239.)

USE #3: REVITALIZE YOUR HOME

Use shades of your favorite and least favorite color to decorate a room so that you feel good about yourself. Color can give you the impetus to become more spiritual, more adventurous, and even more sensual. Consider colors that will make your rooms—and you—come alive. Color has the power to transform your space into a sacred place.

USE #4: ENHANCE YOUR WARDROBE

Before you start on your shopping adventure, consider your favorite colors as your main palette. Be adventurous and accessorize with shades of your least favorite color. You'll evoke empowering agendas. Tell the world who you are.

NOW WHAT DO I DO?

First, your favorite primary color, together with your favorite secondary color, reveals how you see yourself. Self-knowledge is empowering. From it comes the confidence to do what you do best. *Pay attention to your thoughts.* What passionate part of yourself are you able to express? Not able to express?

Remember, don't be in a rush! If you read this book too quickly, you won't be able to absorb everything it has to offer. So relax and get ready to take a passionate journey inside yourself. Turn the page and discover who you are.

PRIMARY CATEGORY
Select your favorite and least favorite

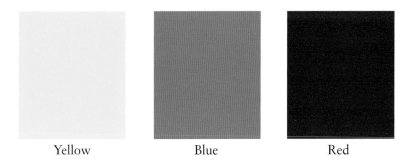

Yellow   Blue   Red

SECONDARY CATEGORY
Select your favorite and least favorite

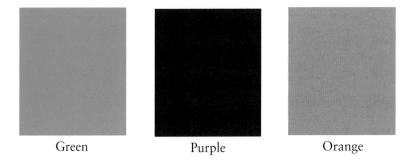

Green   Purple   Orange

ACHROMATIC CATEGORY
Select your favorite and least favorite

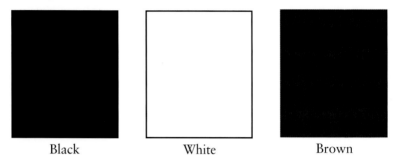

Black   White   Brown

INTERMEDIATE CATEGORY
Select your two favorites and two least favorites

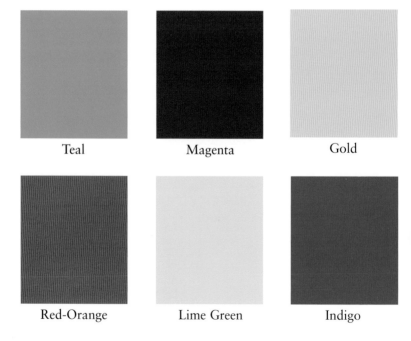

Teal   Magenta   Gold

Red-Orange   Lime Green   Indigo

IS THE "WORK" YOU DIFFERENT
THAN THE "ROMANTIC" YOU?

Certain color combinations have one personality at work and another in their personal relationships. If you are one of these combinations, you'll finally understand the duality of your dynamic personality.

If you choose these favorite primary and secondary combinations—yellow and purple, blue and orange, or red and green—you'll be asked to select another color to understand the romantic you. For example, if you choose red and green, you'll be asked to select again among these color choices: yellow, blue, purple, and orange. If you select purple, you relate to others as a red-purple. In essence, you become a *purple* instead of a *green* in relationships.

Your original primary and secondary combinations represent only your initial response and motivation. Your new combination reflects how you relate to others—your romantic side.

If you select brown as your favorite achromatic color, you'll also be asked to choose again to understand your relationship type. So if you choose red, purple, and brown, you'll be asked, "Do you prefer black or white?" If you choose black, you're a red-purple-black. If you prefer white, you're a red-purple-white. Then read your relationship tips, in the red and purple chapter, for red-purple-black or red-purple-white.

Brown represents that neutral space within you where you assemble facts. Your preference of black or white indicates your commitment style in personal relationships.

Part Two

*Using the System
to Reveal Who You
Really Are*

CHAPTER FOUR

Yellow and Green

The Caretakers

HOW YOU SEE YOURSELF

Your realistic perspective creates comfortable and secure environments for yourself and those around you. You listen to what others say and see their point of view. By questioning what people really need instead of accepting what they think they need, you help them learn.

Taking care of other people is your purpose and natural talent. However, when you're overprotective, you're not doing anyone any favors. Don't interfere with others' abilities to discover their own needs. Constantly rescuing people denies them the opportunity to confront their own responsibilities. So step back and allow them to be themselves without your support. If they should fail, that's okay. Only then will they be able to determine what they ought to be doing.

Since you sympathize with the perspectives of the people in your life, it can be difficult for you to be objective about yourself. Try to forget about your surroundings and focus on your own needs. This will enable others to give you better support and keep you from neglecting your own happiness.

If you like yellow more than green, you are more realistic about your own personal growth and career advancement than you are about your relationships.

If you like green more than yellow, you tend to be more realistic about your relationships and less directed about achieving your goals.

YOUR ENERGY TYPE: HOW OTHERS SEE YOU

Now that you have read the "How You See Yourself" section, add your favorite achromatic selection (black, white, or brown) to your primary and secondary color choices to determine your energy type and understand how others see you.

> Read your energy-type profile with a friend.
> Many times your friend's comments will give you a
> clearer view of yourself. Keep in mind we are not
> necessarily who we think we are.

Yellow, Green, and Black: The Truth Seekers

DISCOVER YOURSELF

You are constantly reexamining yourself to identify what is important. Being truthful is your purpose in life. You need veracity to be aware of yourself. You will speak the truth even when others do not want to listen. When you first meet people, they have no idea that this is who you are. After listening to them, you can't help but be open and honest. You stun them with your obvious truths.

DIVE IN

If you make up your mind about something, there is nothing that can stop you from achieving your goals. You are able to remain focused and resourceful at the same time. By maintaining a keen awareness, you know what is working. This is your great talent. Concentrate on building a trusting rapport with others instead of dwelling on how you are different. Others will feel secure with the advice that you give them, and you will be able to recognize your own emotional patterns in the future.

BUT BEWARE

When people are unwilling to listen, they may reject your ideas or avoid you. Don't feel that you're misunderstood or that you're an outcast. Others are just trying to protect themselves. Accept that you are someone who must tell the truth and that many times others are not strong enough to confront the realities you reveal.

RELATIONSHIP TIPS

Your intense, high-energy personality is somewhat hidden in a crowd. Strangers will see you as honest and open. You need a cause, and you usually find it in being there for someone.

If you choose blue as your least favorite primary color, you are dedicated to giving support to the people in your life who really need you. You are a great friend. Your objective opinions are remarkably accurate. In fact, they can shock those around you so forcefully that they fail to see how much you care. Before you express yourself, tell others, "I have a thought that might help." They will then be better able to understand the way you show love.

If you choose red as your least favorite primary color, you are seeking to be respected. At first you hide who you are, then suddenly reveal yourself to others as a strong, opinionated person they had no idea existed. You are a character! Even though your truthful, well-thought-out statements need to be uttered, you become overly sensitive when others frown at your remarks. Direct your truths at those who are really available to listen. Their positive response will give you the respect that you deserve.

WORK TIPS

You need to be respected as an authority at whatever you do. Use your directness to educate people on how to perform their jobs better and to increase productivity. When others realize you have their best interests at heart, they will respect your talents. You're at your best when you are regularly securing new and better worlds for those around you. Careers in such fields as residential architecture, real estate, medicine, or counseling will make you feel more complete.

THINGS WILL BE JUST FINE IF . . .

. . . prior to giving advice, you consider whether people are in the frame of mind to listen. If they aren't, stop talking. Make a mental note and try having the conversation at another time, using a less emotional way of making your point. Eventually, you will be heard and the truth will come out.

Yellow, Green, and White: The Designers

DISCOVER YOURSELF

You create new ways of improving environments. Your awareness of others and your surroundings allows you to assemble better supportive structures. You design new systems and ways of bettering work or living situations.

An environment with fewer rules will give you the flexibility to see new perspectives. In this world, you can identify each item or resource in your surroundings that makes you or others more comfortable. You will feel that burst of spiritual freedom you are seeking.

DIVE IN

You enjoy assessing the environment, and look for the best options. Since you do not form opinions easily, you often change your point of view and modify your goals with each step of a task. Take advantage of your flexibility to change as situations evolve. Make your fact-based suggestions work.

BUT BEWARE

You sense when others are in the mood to hear what needs to be said. This is a talent. Why bother talking to someone who is not going to listen? Knowing when you are being listened to allows you to make changes in even the most difficult situations or with the most stubborn people.

RELATIONSHIP TIPS

You are a flexible, sensitive lover, friend, or parent. You are very considerate. You will not rest until you know that everyone around you is okay. Make sure you tell people what you need. Otherwise, you may feel as though you're doing for everyone else and getting nothing back.

If you choose blue as your least favorite primary color, your emotional commitment to others pulls your life together. You have an amazing ability to see what others need to make their lives work. This is your great contribution. Take a close look at what you gain from your various interactions. You'll see how you are progressing in your relationships. You will become closer to those you love.

If you choose red as your least favorite primary color, your lack of directness can hide the real you, making it very difficult for others to know how to support you. When you are being supportive of others, make sure you tell them what you need as well. You and everyone you interact with will feel more important in your relationships.

WORK TIPS

Your communication skills are a tremendous asset in today's workforce. You understand other people's perspectives. Adopting that viewpoint helps you express your thoughts diplomatically. You help others appreciate new approaches and different possibilities. This tears down barriers.

When you're at your best, you bring respect for the individual and a sense of integrity to a conversation. Interior decorating, real estate, career counseling, computer programming, travel planning, or any job where you can recommend how to construct a more supportive world would be best for you.

THINGS WILL BE JUST FINE IF . . .

. . . you stop always considering what else others need and focus, instead, on what you need.

Yellow, Green, and Brown: The Givers

DISCOVER YOURSELF

You have a tremendous capacity to experience different people and situations and make them part of your own psyche. By recognizing where there's a need for greater balance, you become aware of what others need to exist. This makes it easy for you to create nurturing environments that allow you and others to live more in the moment and feel more alive.

Your support heals and grounds others, enabling them to be open to your insights about what they need. In turn, this allows them to be themselves. Your very essence is to be needed and to give to others a better world in which to live. Through giving to others, you heal yourself.

DIVE IN

Use your highly realistic perspective to learn how to improve your environment. Recognize the needs of others by studying their actions. Tell them what is necessary for them to do. Your quiet strength allows others to trust you and to let you know who they are. This gives you the ability to recommend things to them. You are recognized as a very giving person, even though you probably don't think so.

BUT BEWARE

If you feel that you are being selfish, you are not in an environment that is supportive of your abilities. Don't be a victim. Get tough with people who do not appreciate you. Show them how much you do. Your hard work must command respect. Otherwise, you will burn out, become defensive, and hide all the love and concern that you have to give.

RELATIONSHIP TIPS

To understand your energy in a relationship, you need to select another achromatic color. Do you prefer black or white? After you've selected your preference, turn to the appropriate page to read your personalized relationship tips.

If you prefer black, you're a yellow-green-black (see page 30). If you prefer white, you're a yellow-green-white (see page 33).

WORK TIPS

Dedication allows you to direct and focus your energy. But you'll get ahead in your career only if you are allowed to be important. Recognition gives you the strength to know how to fix things and give support even before others ask for it. Action-oriented jobs where you can be an expert—a doctor, nurse, physical therapist, or chiropractor—are ones you would enjoy. The more you are needed, the more fun your job will be.

THINGS WILL BE JUST FINE IF . . .

. . . you accept that you have a great need to be appreciated. Direct your concerns to those who care about you. Only then will you be able to acknowledge and take more pride in what you contribute.

CHAPTER FIVE

Yellow and Purple

The Catalysts

HOW YOU SEE YOURSELF

You are on a journey to discover your passion for life. Change fuels your inner fire. First you experience your environment, and then you stand back and analyze it. This sparks your growth and your concerns. You see the value of each moment and have fun when you're committed to personal growth.

Your knowledge of spiritual truths inspires others to discover their own spirituality. Your curious, investigative nature enhances your intuitive powers. You help others to become self-aware. By actively listening, making clever observations, and expressing your feelings, you spark the passions of others to initiate positive change.

You are a great communicator. You have the ability to listen without bias, and understand the possibilities of what could be. During conversations, you are a powerhouse. You see right through things and grasp the real essence of what needs to be done. You are at your best, personally and professionally, when you are communicating.

However, in your obsession with change, you become too concerned about the issues and items of your world. Use your natural talent to know what is real yet see the possibilities. Simply believe in yourself, and you will make the right move. You know how to make positive changes.

If you like yellow more than purple, you first consider the reality of a situation, then you see the possibilities.

If you like purple more than yellow, you consider the possibilities for other people and things before you consider your own future.

YOUR ENERGY TYPE: HOW OTHERS SEE YOU

Now that you have read the "How You See Yourself" section, add your favorite achromatic selection (black, white, or brown) to your primary and secondary color choices to determine your energy type and understand how others see you.

> Read your energy-type profile with a friend. Many times your friend's comments will give you a clearer view of yourself. Keep in mind we are not necessarily who we think we are.

Yellow, Purple, and Black: The Facilitators

DISCOVER YOURSELF

You seek to know about spiritual values, to understand better the meaning of life and to create a sense of purpose. You analyze each feeling you encounter and try to envision possibilities. Your intense interest allows you to focus on getting things done.

Your strong intuitive nature also gives you the ability

to understand what others need for personal growth. You judge people by the quality of their hearts and their spiritual potential, not their possessions or status. You create an understanding of the inner self.

DIVE IN

You have the power to inspire others, and to experience others' feelings as if they were your own. Without even knowing it, you will entice them to find their spiritual selves. Your concern paves the way for them to feel secure enough to explore their interests. You make it okay for them to be themselves.

BUT BEWARE

At times, your intensity toward personal growth can actually impede your progress. Intensity works better when it is directed outward, not inward. Don't let guilt-ridden thoughts deplete your energy. Set emotional boundaries that protect you from becoming too immersed in yourself or in other people's situations. Compulsive concerns can be a defense used to avoid your own problems.

RELATIONSHIP TIPS

To understand your energy in a relationship, you need to select another color. Do you prefer blue, red, green, or orange? After you've selected your preference, turn to the appropriate page to read your personalized relationship tips.

If you prefer blue, you're a blue-purple-black (see page 62); red, you're a red-purple-black (see page 86); green, you're a yellow-green-black (see page 30); orange, you're a yellow-orange-black (see page 46).

WORK TIPS

Your investigative, focused personality gives you the opportunity to be an expert in your chosen field. You desire to experience and analyze. Learning is your motivation, not money. Doing and experiencing new things means everything to you.

And yes, you are a people person. You can regenerate yourself and allow others to be the gems that they are. A few careers that will work for you are medicine, law, or data analysis.

THINGS WILL BE JUST FINE IF . . .

. . . you recognize, for the most part, where your actions are repeating routines, and you are simply viewing the same thing over and over from a different point of view. This will give you a clear perspective of yourself.

Yellow, Purple and White: The Spiritual Wizards

DISCOVER YOURSELF

You are on a journey to investigate who and what really matters in your life. In the beginning, everything seems to work. After a while, though, you are better able to recognize the focal point of your passions. Then you begin to question if you might be happier elsewhere, with different people or in different situations.

You are steadily trying to balance yourself by seeking new options for your spirit. New things allow you to express your inner energy. You like to do lots of things to see how it feels. You are having fun when your environment is changing all the time. Isn't this how you create more passion in your relationships and other situations?

DIVE IN

You know what people need in order to grow. Be the inspiring force that you are, and make suggestions for others to improve their lives. Create better reasons to learn and live, as well as new spiritual perspectives that help you see hidden truths. Use your excellent communication skills to empower others to make their lives more genuine. Be the spiritual wizard that this world so dearly needs.

BUT BEWARE

Forever pondering what to do can hinder your growth. You can become so busy that you lose your ability to set priorities for yourself. Your world can seem to fall apart.

Trust your own beliefs about what would improve things. You'll find that you are usually right. Don't get distracted. Your power for making suggestions about how to create inner passion is too vital not to be unleashed.

RELATIONSHIP TIPS

To understand your energy in a relationship, you need to select another color. Do you prefer blue, red, green, or orange? After you've selected your preference, turn to the appropriate page to read your personal relationship tips.

If you prefer blue, you're a blue-purple-white (see page 64); red, you're a red-purple-white (see page 88); green, you're a yellow-green-white (see page 33); orange, you're a yellow-orange-white (see page 48).

WORK TIPS

Your career decisions are based on personal growth. You focus on how much you are going to learn. You prefer nonrepetitive jobs where you are always being asked to see fresh perspectives. New things energize you. They reinforce your confidence.

You can do almost any job that involves constant change. Fast-growing companies and project-oriented settings where no workday resembles the one before will turn you on. You need to respect the people for whom you work. After all, you must believe in someone before you can learn from him or her.

THINGS WILL BE JUST FINE IF . . .

. . . you celebrate personal victories. Acknowledge how you have helped others to be more passionate. Your personal power will become even greater. You will see exactly who you are, and you will understand how to regenerate your own passion.

Yellow, Purple, and Brown: The Shamans

DISCOVER YOURSELF

Knowing what you want and when you want it gives you spiritual freedom. It fuels your desire to heal yourself and others. Expressing passion gives your spirit the ability to rebuild a wounded soul.

You are aware of the spiritual energy around you. You touch people in a profound, life-altering way. Without their suspecting it, you give people the awareness to declare their inner passions. You're a spiritual healer.

DIVE IN

Encourage situations that are positive. Use your power to identify and eliminate those that are not. It may be as simple as recognizing who is having fun and who is not, or asking the right questions to help everyone understand what's going on.

Very few have the level of awareness that you do. So warn people who are in jeopardy of losing their passions, and help them mend things before it's too late.

BUT BEWARE

Your need to experience life at such a high volume makes it difficult for others to notice your merits. They may feel your advice is too personal, and they may not be able to hear what you have to say.

Remind yourself about your contributions, and recognize what you accomplish with every action you take. Otherwise, you will lose your motivation, and it will be difficult to complete important things. Your kind, giving nature is too valuable to be hidden deep inside of you.

RELATIONSHIP TIPS

To understand your energy in a relationship, you first need to select another color. Do you prefer blue, red, green, or orange?

If you prefer blue, you're a blue-purple. Red, you're a red-purple. Green, you're a yellow-green. Orange, you're a yellow-orange.

Now you need to select another achromatic color. Do you prefer black or white? After you've selected your preference, turn to the appropriate page to read your personalized relationship tips.

If you prefer black, add this new color to what you learned above to become a blue-purple-black (see page 62), red-purple-black (see page 86), yellow-green-black (see page 30), or a yellow-orange-black (see page 46). If you prefer white, you become a blue-purple-white (see page 64), red-purple-white (see page 88), yellow-green-white (see page 33), or a yellow-orange-white (see page 48).

WORK TIPS

Choose an environment in which you can do your own thing in conjunction with someone else. You gravitate toward people who will teach you through new experiences. You know opportunity when you see it. Experiencing new situations is a thrill. They enable you to learn how to fit better into the world around you.

Take advantage of your ability to make things work. You will enjoy high-activity professions where you are part of a team or participate in expansive technologies such as computer systems.

THINGS WILL BE JUST FINE IF . . .

. . . you tell those you care about how dedicated you are to them. Doing for others is not enough. They must hear about your feelings in your own words. Your friends will then remind you of how much you give to them. This will regenerate your spirit.

CHAPTER SIX

Yellow and Orange

The Technical Thinkers

HOW YOU SEE YOURSELF

Your first thoughts are about how to get things done. By establishing a systematic approach, you better understand tasks, relationships, even life. Your realism makes others see you as technical. You see yourself as one who maximizes resources.

You playfully examine the talents and resources around you. Your experimental approach allows the world to reveal itself to you. Your discoveries give you the power to put talents and resources to better use.

Fun, to you, means being emotionally committed to investigating how all the facts fit together. You examine successful parts of a task or relationship as if you were putting together a puzzle. Each piece is a resource or a personal value that can be used to make something new, or to reinvent a relationship. To the amazement of others, you create something original from what already exists.

Under pressure, your technical approach helps you to see what has not been done. This can make others defensive. They see you as being formal or rigid. Since you are usually the first to notice when someone has made a mistake, you make people worry.

Be especially careful if you are in an unstimulating environment. Without new information steadily coming in, you can find yourself in a rut. Others will view you as negative or nitpicking. In actuality, you feel lost and are searching to find what you want.

If you like yellow more than orange, your own personal growth comes before your relationships.

If you like orange more than yellow, you think of what others need before you think of yourself.

YOUR ENERGY TYPE: HOW OTHERS SEE YOU

Now that you have read the "How You See Yourself" section, add your favorite achromatic selection (black, white, or brown) to your primary and secondary color choices to determine your energy type and understand how others see you.

> Read your energy-type profile with a friend. Many times your friend's comments will give you a clearer view of yourself. Keep in mind we are not necessarily who we think we are.

Yellow, Orange, and Black: The Inventors

DISCOVER YOURSELF

You are able to shape your varied experiences into something cohesive. Technical information and diverse projects are pooled together and are used for future inventions. You have the unusual combination of being able to work with both people and things. You enjoy living fast, but you slow down to process information and make long-term decisions. This change in gears helps you get what you want.

DIVE IN

You're an innovator, far ahead of anyone else when it comes to both people and projects. You have the ability to create something from nothing by reinventing the resources around you. When your thinking is direct and intense, new ideas and possibilities arrive with a bang. Set your mind on something, and nothing will stop you. Your know-how is unparalleled.

BUT BEWARE

When people first meet you, they are not aware of your warmth. Instead, they get caught up in your defenses. Once they see the personable, vulnerable you, they will become aware of your needs and their importance in your life.

RELATIONSHIP TIPS

Your exciting, magnetic persona is hard to ignore when you enter a room. You are a very inventive and fun person. Others get to know your sensitive side by your efforts on their behalf. You create liveliness where it is needed. You especially enjoy turning the most boring situation or mundane routine into a party. When you create positive change, you're at your best.

If you choose blue as your least favorite primary color, your commitment to change pulls your life together. You use your On and Off switches to set boundaries. This allows you to protect your heart. Be careful. When you become overconcerned with your thoughts, you can lose your ability to see the big picture.

If you choose red as your least favorite primary color, you are seeking respect. Though initially you hide who you are, soon others are confronted by a strong individual they had no idea existed. You are an enigma. Despite all your achievements, you can feel wounded if others frown at your boldness. Direct your energy toward people who care enough to listen to you. Their positive responses and respect are what you deserve.

WORK TIPS

Use your abilities to encourage people and construct new things by pulling together the resources and talents around you. You are a natural at technical work. You're also a great motivator of people. Use both these assets, and you will feel complete. Your people skills and technical abilities accommodate a wide range of careers.

THINGS WILL BE JUST FINE IF . . .

. . . you stop going through life with a ready-made checklist. Otherwise, even those you love will perceive themselves as unimportant, merely items on a long grocery list.

Yellow, Orange, and White: The Information Junkies

DISCOVER YOURSELF

You seek information to gain self-recognition. You take things apart to analyze how they are made, and then wonder why they weren't made another way. You try to concentrate on learning pertinent facts and are aware that what is now in vogue will eventually become dated. This appreciation keeps you on the cusp. You are the first to know the latest information.

You are the lightest color combination and the most undefined in the entire color spectrum. You easily become a part of any situation. You mold your behavior in order to fit in with those around you. Without conflict and barriers, you can receive more information.

DIVE IN

Observe the options and resources available. Your methodical way of analyzing facts is your great talent. Continually making suggestions about available options, you can concentrate on the facts regardless of life's pressures. Your knowledge makes everyone's life easier to endure, less emotionally erratic, and more about what is important.

BUT BEWARE

Don't get caught up in making plans and agendas and then fail to act on them. When you get too intense and are overloaded with information, it becomes difficult for you to think clearly. Others can see you as not having a clear focus in life.

RELATIONSHIP TIPS

Your energetic, vivacious, and inquisitive personality is tuned in to everyone around you. You offer outrageous solutions that often work. When uncomfortable, however, you give too much information. Talk less, and your invaluable advice will gain you the recognition you are seeking.

If you choose blue as your least favorite primary color, your dedication to others pulls your life together and helps you see what they need to improve their lives. This is a great talent. Try to be mindful of what you give. Appreciating yourself will make you closer to those you love.

If you choose red as your least favorite primary color, you have a great need to be respected by your peers. But don't put on airs or hide behind knowledge to try to impress people. You'll make it difficult for people to appreciate you for what you have to say. When you are giving advice to others, try not to neglect your own feelings. The more sincere you are, the closer your relationships will be.

WORK TIPS

By analyzing numbers and information, you know whether or not something will work. You'll thrive at jobs where you can rely on your factual expertise. Consider working with computers, research, or being a librarian.

Don't be subtle when correcting coworkers or giving them instructions. Being firm will help them see why things have to be done a certain way. Only after they have spent time around you will they get used to your low-key criticism.

THINGS WILL BE JUST FINE IF . . .

. . . you dwell longer on the nuances that you are considering. Otherwise, in your quest for new information, you'll become lost in all the details.

Yellow, Orange, and Brown: The Troubleshooters

DISCOVER YOURSELF

You're the one who makes sure that everything is working, whether it has to do with the lives of friends or with something mechanical, such as a noisy engine. You have the ability to see the needs of others and understand just what you are capable of doing to help. When you are committed and loyal to someone, you help him recognize his strengths.

DIVE IN

You have the ability to create a world in which others can have more passion. Your high energy level and intense living style wake up even the dullest moments. You offer a perfect example of how to live.

Use your ability to see how things work to regenerate your relationships and other situations. Focus on how everything fits together. You will give others a better understanding of their everyday processes and increase their ability to enjoy the individual moments of their lives. This fresh perspective is your forte.

BUT BEWARE

Guard against becoming too immersed in what you are doing. If you lose sight of your objective, you will lose your creativity and yourself. Hold on to your future by staying committed to your overall plan. Don't sound the fire alarm when you intuitively identify the negative actions of others. Allow folks more time. People are simply not as aware of the significance of their actions as you are.

RELATIONSHIP TIPS

To understand your energy in a relationship, you need to select another achromatic color. Do you prefer black or white? After you've selected your preference, turn to the appropriate page to read your personalized relationship tips.

If you prefer black, you're a yellow-orange-black (see

page 46); if you prefer white, you're a yellow-orange-white (see page 48).

WORK TIPS

You clearly understand people's contributions. Use your ability to distinguish the doers from the talkers. No matter how anyone tries to get the emotional edge on you, that's not going to happen. Use your exactness to ensure that the facts are the primary consideration.

You'll thrive at jobs that allow you to concentrate on the nuts and bolts and to fix things. Avoid work environments in which you're forced to deal with abstract concepts.

THINGS WILL BE JUST FINE IF . . .

. . . you make people aware of your accomplishments. This will help you to see who really believes in your abilities. Otherwise, your dedication can falter and you can lose focus.

CHAPTER SEVEN

Blue and Green

The Anchors

HOW YOU SEE YOURSELF

You have fun nurturing and supporting others. Your endless curiosity entices them to tell you what they are thinking. You see people's dreams and are sensitive to their needs. You give them the self-confidence to believe in their own capabilities. Your concerns for them make them feel important. Your listening grounds them.

At first, you have a need to fit in. Others can assume you are like them. Then the real you appears. Now they must reacquaint themselves with a person they thought they already knew. This authentic you might have less in common with them than they believed. Because of this disparity, you sometimes attract situations and relationships that don't provide you with what you need.

You listen intensely. You want to know how others feel. This gives you the ability to hear music and languages better. If the opportunity is available, you can play an instrument well and speak your native language or other languages with less of an accent. You are articulate.

When you become too comfortable or too earnest, you

neglect your personal growth and relationships. Be more conclusive about what you expect. Then others will know how to meet your needs, and your life will be more pleasing.

If you like blue more than green, your career or personal goals are your first priority. Your relationships need to agree with your dreams.

If you like green more than blue, you're supportive of others' dreams before your own.

YOUR ENERGY TYPE: HOW OTHERS SEE YOU

Now that you have read the "How You See Yourself" section, add your favorite achromatic selection (black, white, or brown) to your primary and secondary color choices to determine your energy type and understand how others see you.

> Read your energy-type profile with a friend.
> Many times your friend's comments will give you a
> clearer view of yourself. Keep in mind we are not
> necessarily who we think we are.

Blue, Green, and Black: The Identity Creators

DISCOVER YOURSELF

You are in touch with your emotions and clearly express what you want. When you listen to the concerns of others, you discover what is best for them. You help them accept themselves. They learn about things that they have deeply internalized and are afraid to face. You strengthen their identity. You give to others the gift of better self-knowledge.

DIVE IN

You can intuit others' hopes and fears by their tone of voice. Engage others in conversation so that you can help them discover what they need. Take your concerns for them and translate them into supportive suggestions. Keeping each person or situation on track is your greatest talent. It allows you to determine your own identity as well.

BUT BEWARE

You have a great need for others to hear you as well as you hear them. If you become frustrated, you ask others questions about decisions that you've already made. In your search to confirm your feelings, you can make people feel that you're uninterested in their comments about you. They perceive that you are not listening to what they say. You do hear them. It just takes you longer to process information about your feelings.

RELATIONSHIP TIPS

Your attractive appearance and attentive disposition are very alluring. Your puppy-dog eyes express real concern. You love to be doted on. Your thoughts are about being supported or supporting others. This makes you a natural in relationships. You have a sincere love for those around you. This is one of your greatest powers.

If you choose yellow as your least favorite primary color, you see others as who they believe themselves to be. Beware. You can attract someone who does not respect your concerns. Don't be so stubborn. Make sure your expectations are realistic before you set your heart on another person.

If you choose red as your least favorite primary color, you appear very vulnerable. This gives you the power to be very seductive. Others have a need to give you whatever you want. The problem is that they do not have a clue about you, let alone what you really want. Speak up more.

WORK TIPS

Be sensitive to the emotions of your coworkers and be supportive. This is a responsibility that you rightly claim. If you are a manager, appreciate your ability to remain dedicated to your staff, and you will gain strong employee commitment and loyalty. Be careful. If you get too close to those you work with, you will be unable to give unbiased guidance. You work best in environments in which you are consistently working with new clients or situations.

Careers that allow you to hear and express how others feel are a must for you. Working as a writer, actor, psychologist, psychiatrist, manager, or designer of support systems will allow you to use your natural talents.

THINGS WILL BE JUST FINE IF . . .

. . . you stop compulsively talking about or considering what is not working for you. Dwelling on nonsupportive situations or relationships too long can stop you from moving forward.

Blue, Green, and White: The Intellectuals

DISCOVER YOURSELF

Your objective point of view helps people to understand what they need to have a more balanced life. Your straightforward, unbiased comments make it easy for others to hear you. They understand that you're genuinely motivated to make their lives better. Improving the status quo sparks your inner passion.

DIVE IN

You have astute common sense, even in difficult situations where others lose their cool. By staying concerned and objective, you have the power to recommend solutions. This is your natural talent. You can keep your distance, yet maintain your concern. People's faith in you gives you the inner strength to believe more in yourself.

BUT BEWARE

When you're upset, you put distance between yourself and those who rely on you. This can make you seem aloof, and people may start to question whether you believe in them. If you don't let others know who you are and how you feel, they will become remote and feel as though they are unimportant in your life. You can drive away people who treasure, love, and support you the most.

RELATIONSHIP TIPS

You get others interested in you by giving them your undivided attention. Then you appear unavailable. Some might find this enticing, but it will be difficult for them to get close to you. Intimacy can make you uncomfortable after a while. You require information about people before you can get close to them.

If you choose yellow as your least favorite primary color, you appear to be very open and endearing. Others can feel that you have a need to be loved. Then you become unavailable. Aren't you logically justifying whether the relationship in question is of value to you? Be careful. Keep your concerns focused on those you love.

If you choose red as your least favorite primary color, others see you as very mysterious and flirtatious. Initially you enjoy mental stimulation. However, you can find yourself in relationships where there is very little physical chemistry. Your emotions can be saying yes, while you are thinking no. If there's sexual attraction, there is real potential for a solid relationship. You will still be curious about all the options available. Who else would you like to be with? How would it feel?

WORK TIPS

You are at your best when you are recommending easier ways of doing things. You don't become obsessed with the need to realize the final goal. Your neutral perspective enables you to teach, perform managerial duties, or work for large corporations.

THINGS WILL BE JUST FINE IF . . .

. . . you communicate your need for space, then take the time to discern which relationships and situations are vital to you.

Blue, Green, and Brown: The Dream Makers

DISCOVER YOURSELF

You experience a sense of personal harmony when you help people. Your capacity to listen and offer suggestions allows them to become more aware of what they need. They gain a balanced perspective. You avoid extremes and use facts to improve situations. You know how to make others' dreams come true by taking the appropriate action.

DIVE IN

Your clear understanding of the needs of people gives you a realistic approach to your relationships and your environment. Use your natural talent to promote people and causes. Take on other people's burdens as if they were your own. You will create new worlds that benefit everyone. You are the dream maker.

BUT BEWARE

In a crisis where things can be overwhelming, you become overly concerned with what others need. You end up feeling deprived and overreact by doing what you want to do regardless of what is expected. This can lead to your destroying things that you will miss later. Being too nice and then too selfish can make it difficult for others to appreciate all the good you do.

RELATIONSHIP TIPS

To understand your behavior in a relationship, you need to select another achromatic color. Do you prefer black or white?

If you prefer black, you're a blue-green-black (see page 54); white, you're a blue-green-white (see page 56). After you've selected your preference, turn to the appropriate page to read your personalized relationship tips.

WORK TIPS

The more you participate, the more fun your job will be. You enjoy creating environments that allow others to be

hopeful about the future. Acknowledge your ability to perform tasks. Act with positive energy. People will feel your
inner fire and be motivated to act.

You are at your best when you are supporting people
through periods of crisis or fixing things. You see life from a
physical, supportive perspective. You'd enjoy working as a
doctor, nurse, physical therapist, corporate trainer, chiropractor, or carpenter.

THINGS WILL BE JUST FINE IF . . .

. . . you stop being so dedicated to others and tell them
what you need. Your life will become fun again.

CHAPTER EIGHT

Blue and Purple

The Thinkers

HOW YOU SEE YOURSELF

You ponder existence. You need to know why things are. The conclusions you come to allow you to see the big picture. Your understanding of what is needed enables you to make improvements. By focusing on the future, you think of ideas and things as if they were already completed. You live in this future vision. It's a picture in your head.

You are at your best when you understand human motivation and the laws of cause and effect. You are constantly categorizing things to create plans of action. Without these plans, it can be difficult for you to be organized. You become a scattered daydreamer.

You are a trailblazer. When you're committed to developing new ideas and structures, you have fun. Making the ideas in your head a reality allows your passions to soar. When your faith is strong, you can assume things, regardless of the truth. False assumptions about yourself or others can throw you off base.

Your constant need to do something new can keep you from appreciating what you have done. Too many pictures in your head can make your life difficult. Situations or other people will not measure up. Unknowingly, you can ask for the unattainable, especially from yourself.

If you like blue more than purple, you consider your dreams first and your relationships second.

If you like purple more than blue, you are primarily concerned about how to be more powerful in your existing relationships.

YOUR ENERGY TYPE: HOW OTHERS SEE YOU

Now that you have read the "How You See Yourself" section, add your favorite achromatic selection (black, white, or brown) to your primary and secondary color choices to determine your energy type and understand how others see you.

> Read your energy-type profile with a friend. Many times your friend's comments will give you a clearer view of yourself. Keep in mind we are not necessarily who we think we are.

Blue, Purple, and Black: The Pioneers

DISCOVER YOURSELF

You think about why people do what they do. By understanding the motivation of others, you seek to create a better world. Changing the world around you through personal achievements is your everyday challenge. The constant investigation of feelings, thoughts, and ideas is your passion.

DIVE IN

You are the darkest color in the spectrum. Darkness denotes emotional depth. Use your talents to visualize possibilities. Your ability to picture things clearly in your head helps you perform tasks with very few missteps and minimal risk. Others see this quality as self-confidence. They think you always know what you are doing. Stay focused on the big picture. When you understand the overall concept, there's nothing you can't do.

BUT BEWARE

You will not be able to accomplish things exactly the way you envision them. Be realistic and realize that every process must be constantly revamped and adapted. When you feel emotional about something, stop and take a breath. Chances are, you are ignoring concrete facts or issues. Have you made unrealistic assumptions? Do you see an easier way? No, you can't have everything you expected, but you can have most of it.

RELATIONSHIP TIPS

The romantic ideas in your head make the world around you delicious. You need to be enveloped by your lover. Forget the practical details. Fantasy is more fun.

If you choose yellow as your least favorite primary color, your dramatic, eccentric flair is sexy. The only problem is that many times you move too fast, and get what you think you want instead of what you really need. Be more cautious and realistic about other people before you get involved. Otherwise, you will be constantly disappointed.

If you choose red as your least favorite primary color, you see the depth and possibilities of each person. This makes you very appealing. You're open to everything. Others love your fun and easygoing style. However, your openness can make you vulnerable. Loving and caring about someone is not about ignoring your own needs. Make a list of criteria you require. Whenever someone or something fails to meet one of them, talk about it.

WORK TIPS

Use your big-picture thinking to develop new markets, new ideas, and new businesses. You see what is missing and know what is required to get things done. You are a great motivator who needs to make an impact and express new ideas. Your dramatic flair helps initiate action. Creative fields such as advertising, marketing, sales, design, trial law, or any area that allows you to investigate the unknown will make you the happiest.

THINGS WILL BE JUST FINE IF . . .

. . . you stop thinking so much. Your obsession with your ideas or planning the way you are going to feel can make it difficult for you to enjoy your life.

Blue, Purple, and White: The Problem Solvers

DISCOVER YOURSELF

You are constantly considering what else each person or situation requires. You want to know what is missing. During the time that you mull things over, others might view you as passive or quiet. When you have assembled all the facts about the situation, you put forward a vibrant suggestion on how to make something or someone's life work better. Solving problems is your greatest passion.

DIVE IN

Examine ideas and situations. Tell others about better ways to solve a problem. Be steadfast. Your method of forcing yourself to work under pressure allows you to be at your best. You can see the idea and critique it until it is perfect. Demand autonomy. You need it to finish what you start. A sharp, successful focus will be your reward.

BUT BEWARE

When you don't know what you want, you can appear wishy-washy to others. It can also make it difficult for you to stay focused. External pressure can destroy your ability to concentrate and be creative.

Make your own plan and take the time to weigh all the options. In order to give yourself some thinking space for problem solving, tell others you will have to get back to them. Later, you can let them know your thoughts on how to resolve difficulties.

RELATIONSHIP TIPS

Your classy style creates romantic possibilities. When you first meet a person, you have no clue if he or she is right for you. Only when you spend time alone together will you know if he or she fits your ideal.

If you choose yellow as your least favorite primary color, your need to know all the answers can make you appear unavailable or somewhat formal. Then all of a sudden others may see you as a very open person. Enjoy the present, instead of obsessing over the future. Others will see your warmth. Who or what you are looking for will appear.

If you choose red as your least favorite primary color, you appear seductive and intriguing and may even evoke a sense of the forbidden. Others will find you very appealing, and may be surprised when later on they see how much logic informs your thinking. Express your feelings, not just your thoughts. Otherwise, you will waste a lot of time and create a lot of frustration.

WORK TIPS

Analyze your options, and use your creativity to transform ideas into reality. Request that you learn why everyone did each task. This will allow your logical mind to fit everything together. You are good at organizing, developing, and creating things. However, too many ideas, agendas, or different topics can make you scattered.

Your advice gives others new perspectives on how to create a better future. You would excel at such jobs as career counseling, public relations, human resources, corporate law, or architecture.

THINGS WILL BE JUST FINE IF . . .

. . . you give yourself the space and time to connect your thoughts. Initially your thinking is rigid, then flexible. On your own you can weave both of these tendencies into a comprehensive plan.

Blue, Purple, and Brown: The Scientific Thinkers

DISCOVER YOURSELF

You hypothesize possibilities. Then you measure them. You passionately investigate new methods to see what works. Your inquisitiveness and methodical approach help you to gain insight into the future of your relationships and other situations.

Your keen awareness and your belief that things will work out give you the dedication to do things in a more thorough way. You recognize, even before things begin, where you can make improvements. You are constantly moving forward, with your feet on the ground, to create a better world.

DIVE IN

Be direct. Take action, and improve the physical world. Use your compulsive need to search for practical solutions to develop even better methods for improving things. When you are dedicated to something, there is no stopping you. You become persistent and aware of each issue that needs to be addressed. Seeing what you have actually accomplished is a must for you.

BUT BEWARE

Your ability to evaluate what each situation or person needs for success is amazing. Your facts make things work. They can be seen, however, as too direct. Others can perceive you as being abrasive. Don't take it personally. Your factual comments are invaluable, even if they upset the status quo. Stay focused on your long-term goals, and seek out environments that give you plenty of autonomy.

RELATIONSHIP TIPS

To understand your energy in a relationship, you need to select another achromatic color. Do you prefer black or white? After you've selected your preference, turn to the appropriate page to read your personalized relationship tips.

If you prefer black, you're a blue-purple-black (see

page 62). If you prefer white, you're a blue-purple-white (see page 64).

WORK TIPS

You have a very realistic understanding of how to get the job done. Your ability to envision new things and see if they work gives you the appearance of a truly calm, analytical, process-oriented person. Doing what you want allows you to create long-term plans.

A few occupations you might consider are scientific research, acting, quality-control management, product design, or gourmet cooking.

THINGS WILL BE JUST FINE IF . . .

. . . you have the freedom to do what you enjoy. Your creations will be personal celebrations.

CHAPTER NINE

Blue and Orange

The Builders

HOW YOU SEE YOURSELF

You demand an exciting life. You create it with your dual personality. One moment you are the innovative freethinker who wishes to construct a new modular home, and the next moment you shift gears and become a traditional critic, questioning why anyone would undertake such a thing. You are a social enigma.

Your curiosity sparks wide-ranging conversations. You thrive on them. This makes you fun at parties. Your friends are a bunch of characters with very diverse interests. Sometimes you stop and wonder how you keep finding yourself amid such craziness. But deep down you know that too much order in a social environment can restrict people's growth.

You want to believe that the world needs you. Often, you become preoccupied with trying to make sense of social situations over which you have no control. In the end, you feel frustrated and emotionally depleted. You must realize that the world is never going to be a perfect place. A person can do only so much, and you will find that you're most effective when you focus on improving your immediate surroundings.

If you're not dedicated to a cause, it's impossible for you to be constructive. When you are in a situation where you cannot give your all, move on. You need to be building something, or you will get depressed.

If you like blue more than orange, you consider how to build something new first, then critique your plan.

If you like orange more than blue, it's easy for you to get caught up in the thrill of the moment and forget your plans.

YOUR ENERGY TYPE: HOW OTHERS SEE YOU

Now that you have read the "How You See Yourself" section, add your favorite achromatic selection (black, white, or brown) to your primary and secondary color choices to determine your energy type and understand how others see you.

> Read your energy-type profile with a friend. Many times your friend's comments will give you a clearer view of yourself. Keep in mind we are not necessarily who we think we are.

Blue, Orange, and Black: The Managers

DISCOVER YOURSELF

Your thoughts are about constructing something new. You are constantly looking at past experiences to see what was of value. Then you tell everyone what actions need to be taken or avoided. Keeping things on the right course is your greatest passion.

DIVE IN

You're an expert at asking pertinent questions. They guide you and others to see what contributes to an optimal goal. You can make people and resources fit together. Use your sharp perception to scrutinize what is important, and you will be able to complete any task that you are given. You have a natural managerial style.

BUT BEWARE

Don't let your intense scrutiny of things slow you down. Prioritize your plans for the future. It will free you of the past without so much effort on your part. Others will find you more lovable and exciting. They will open up to you even further.

RELATIONSHIP TIPS

To understand your energy in a relationship, you need to select another color. Do you prefer yellow, red, green, or purple? After you've selected your preference, turn to the appropriate page to read your personalized relationship tips.

If you prefer yellow, you're a yellow-orange-black (see page 46); red, you're a red-orange-black (see page 94); green, you're a blue-green-black (see page 54); purple, you're a blue-purple-black (see page 62).

WORK TIPS

You direct a task by taking advantage of others' feedback. Your concerned questions make them respect you. You understand that developing something new requires their commitment. The information you derive allows you to better direct projects. You make sure that those who are loyal to you or your company are treated with respect. When you are focused, you are a natural leader.

You'll prefer a busy environment, even if there is stress involved, because you'll enjoy learning. Pressure actually stimulates you. Careers involving task management, overseeing change implementation, value assessment, and analyzing efficiency are best for you.

THINGS WILL BE JUST FINE IF . . .

. . . you do not become overly engrossed in memories. You will gain a vision of how to build a future that provides better for your emotional needs.

Blue, Orange, and White: The Social Investigators

DISCOVER YOURSELF

You learn through watching others or by analyzing how things are made. When you watch others, you're drawn to their energy as if you are watching TV. You see each person's contribution to a common objective. By examining someone's point of view, you see the very depths of his or her motivation. This is how you regularly fine-tune the way you direct your own life.

DIVE IN

Use your excellent eye to examine closely just why your goals are not being realized. Your ability to view situations in great detail lets you see things that no one else could imagine. This is your great talent. You can initiate a plan or introduce something new, critique why it is or isn't working, then offer new perspectives and solutions.

BUT BEWARE

The process of setting goals and analyzing them works better for you in your career than at home. You need to invent your own activities, as opposed to being told what to do. Without the freedom to explore your passions, you can get caught up in an endless cycle of second-guessing yourself. This is dangerous because ultimately you'll wind up talking yourself out of what you really need.

RELATIONSHIP TIPS

To understand your energy in a relationship, you need to select another color. Do you prefer yellow, red, green, or purple? After you've selected your preference, turn to the appropriate page to read your personalized relationship tips.

If you prefer yellow, you're a yellow-orange-white (see page 48); red, you're a red-orange-white (see page 96); green, you're a blue-green-white (see page 56); purple, you're a blue-purple-white (see page 64).

WORK TIPS

You have the power to construct new things in the workplace. You can both initiate change and assess what you have created. Effortlessly, you are able to decide how to direct resources and people. At the start, your strong beliefs make things work. If you get bored or distracted, however, you can lose your ability to complete projects successfully.

Your never-ending suggestions work well in such career fields as the hospitality industry, corporate law, resource management, and employment recruitment.

THINGS WILL BE JUST FINE IF . . .

. . . you slow down. Don't be such a fast thinker. Don't end a conversation until those around you have had their say. Give them the time to understand all the facts so that they will be better able to assist you in realizing a project.

Blue, Orange, and Brown: The Activists

DISCOVER YOURSELF

You're well loved, giving, and affectionate. Maybe the reason for this is that you're dedicated to making the world a better place. You're not just a talker; you're a person of action. You introduce a sense of purpose and caring to your social environment. The activist in you brings people together to work toward improving the future. You have the ability to create hope.

DIVE IN

Embrace your dedication to change the world around you. You are at your best when you are actually doing something that you helped plan. Your strong beliefs and no-nonsense approach make it happen. This style calms people down. It also allows them to believe in you. Your astute awareness is comforting.

BUT BEWARE

When you're upset or under pressure, you may do the wrong thing, even though it feels right at the time. Avoid making rash decisions. Take a moment to relax and have fun. Your inner strength will return. Otherwise, you'll end up betraying the beliefs you hold dear.

RELATIONSHIP TIPS

To understand your energy in a relationship, you first need to select another color. Do you prefer yellow, red, green, or purple? If you prefer yellow, you're a yellow-orange; red, a red-orange; green, a blue-green; and purple, you're a blue-purple.

Now you also need to select another achromatic color. Do you prefer black or white? After you've selected your preference, turn to the appropriate page to read your personalized relationship tips.

If you prefer black, then you're a yellow-orange-black (see page 46), red-orange-black (see page 94), blue-green-black (see page 54), or a blue-purple-black (see page 62). If you prefer white, you're a yellow-orange-white (see page 48), red-orange-white (see page 96), blue-green-white (see page 56), or a blue-purple-white (see page 64).

WORK TIPS

When you are focused on building something, you are at your best. Occupations that allow you to make direct, exact specifications, such as engineering, building, or developing new programs, companies, or products, will challenge you. Also consider jobs in fields where you can make a difference, such as a social work, law enforcement, or firefighting. You need to be involved in lots of activity directed at improving services for those around you in order to feel good about yourself.

THINGS WILL BE JUST FINE IF . . .

. . . you resist instant gratification. The future that you envisioned will be yours.

CHAPTER TEN

Red and Green

The Resource Managers

HOW YOU SEE YOURSELF

Practical and nurturing, you teach others how to achieve more value in their lives. No one fools you. You're a dynamic personality and know exactly what everyone is up to. You've got a knack for knowing what is important. Like a parent or a teacher, you are concerned about how to make people's lives better. Helping others boosts your self-respect.

You are at your best when you are directing the use of resources. You start out very nurturing but become very authoritative and even bossy. There is no middle ground. You are either one or the other. This can be confusing to those around you. People don't always realize that even when you're being bossy you're looking out for their best interests.

When you are upset, under pressure, or intoxicated, you favor your expressive red side. Without the calming effects of green, you can really shock your friends with outrageous behavior. If you like green more than red, this characteristic is even more dramatic. If others act differently toward you during one of your episodes of flamboyant behavior, it is because they feel they don't know you.

If you like red more than green, you consider what things are needed to achieve an objective before you think of other people. This attribute allows you to be direct and confident.

If you like green more than red, your supportive nature wins out and you initially direct your energy toward what other people need.

YOUR ENERGY TYPE: HOW OTHERS SEE YOU

Now that you have read the "How You See Yourself" section, add your favorite achromatic selection (black, white, or brown) to your primary and secondary color choices to determine your energy type and understand how others see you.

> Read your energy-type profile with a friend. Many times your friend's comments will give you a clearer view of yourself. Keep in mind we are not necessarily who we think we are.

Red Green, and Black: The Investors

DISCOVER YOURSELF

By focusing on what others need, you learn the exact value and potential of each person in different situations. You instinctively know how motivated others are in supporting you. This helps you surround yourself with the right people.

Your generous nature gives you a feeling of security. It makes you feel comfortable and in control of your life. You know that a better future can be achieved only by investing in those people who respect you and in projects that have the capability to grow in a positive fashion.

DIVE IN

Appreciate your ability to understand practical realities. By being sensitive to how different people express their emotions, you display your greatest talent. You learn which situations are supportive of other folks and which are not. In fact, you'll see what they need even when they don't know themselves. You make them feel comfortable in your presence, even when they barely know you.

BUT BEWARE

Under pressure you obsess over facts, concern yourself with small matters, and lose sight of the big picture. This makes you so skeptical that you lose perspective and think only about short-term plans. Without a sense of hope for your future, you become overly critical of yourself and aspects of your life. Others can see you as judgmental. In resolving problems, taking a fair-minded tack wins more respect and support than using an all-or-nothing approach.

RELATIONSHIP TIPS

To understand your energy in a relationship, you need to select another color. Do you prefer blue, yellow, purple, or orange? After you've selected your preference, turn to the appropriate page to read your personalized relationship tips.

If you prefer blue, you're a blue-green-black (see page 54); yellow, you're a yellow-green-black (see page 30); purple, you're a red-purple-black (see page 86); orange, you're a red-orange-black (see page 94).

WORK TIPS

Appreciate your ability to know when support is needed and where money can be best spent. You can excel in careers that place a high emphasis upon the optimal use of resources.

Consider fields such as finance, accounting, banking, manufacturing, property management, production analysis, investment, money management, consulting, architecture, selling a product, or teaching personal development. You will do well wherever you can be nurturing and direct.

THINGS WILL BE JUST FINE IF . . .

. . . you know that people recognize your kindness, concern, and accomplishments. You will find the respect and self-esteem you are seeking.

Red, Green, and White: The Practical Wizards

DISCOVER YOURSELF

You understand what people need to do to be more practical in their lives. By keeping your distance, you are able to identify the best available resources. You're constantly conducting an investigation of how to better use money and to cultivate talent. Then, much to your amazement, solutions seem to appear out of nowhere. Your objective, practical perspective can turn a disaster into a rousing success.

DIVE IN

You have the power to know what points of view, resources, and approaches are needed. Your practical thoughts and considerations make the best of what you have. You combine talents or information to attain goals. Use your ability to assess things critically and create powerful change in people's lives. Those who believe in you will gain new opportunities.

BUT BEWARE

You send confusing messages to others. One moment people can see you as a person who makes them feel very important to you; the next moment they feel that you see them as just numbers. When you become absorbed in your search for new options, people can sense that you have forgotten that they were there for you. Help them to understand your need to take a step back in order to solve problems. It will keep them on your team while you sort out all the facts.

RELATIONSHIP TIPS

To understand your energy in a relationship, you need to select another color. Do you prefer blue, yellow, purple, or orange? After you've selected your preference, turn to the appropriate page to read your personalized relationship tips.

If you prefer blue, you're a blue-green-white (see page 56); yellow, you're a yellow-green-white (see page 32); purple, you're a red-purple-white (see page 88); orange, you're a red-orange-white (see page 96).

WORK TIPS

Your logical, supportive perspective is often in demand. You understand the underlying premise of things and work best when challenged by new points of view. Look for environments in which you can come into contact with different types of people and situations.

Jobs that involve compilation of facts, such as training, career development, organization of tasks, auditing, or marketing, will allow you to express your energy.

THINGS WILL BE JUST FINE IF . . .

. . . you recognize the value of change. New experiences help bolster your self-esteem and give you the self-confidence to focus on what is right in your life.

Red, Green, and Brown: The Crusaders

DISCOVER YOURSELF

You bring out the best in people. You help them accept their limitations and abilities. Giving them a good dose of reality keeps them grounded. Your crusade is to develop people's self-awareness and make their dreams a reality.

DIVE IN

Use your high energy level to make many improvements in the course of a day. Once you know what you want, go get it! Turn everyday needs into causes to champion. You can be a little tornado. When you direct your energy inward, you are a tower of strength. When you turn that energy toward others, you are a giver; when you turn it toward goals, you are a practical director.

BUT BEWARE

You need to be cautious about your frantic schedule. You can get so carried away with thoughts of supporting others that you push yourself too far, both emotionally and physically. Excessive responsibilities will eventually destroy your passion and make you enraged. When you become burned out, you can become lazy and demoralized. Allow yourself to relax. This will restore your energy and help you bounce back with a renewed, dedicated spirit.

RELATIONSHIP TIPS

To understand your energy in a relationship, you first need to select another color. Do you prefer yellow, blue, orange, or purple? If you prefer yellow, you're a yellow-green; blue, a blue-green; purple, a red-purple; orange, a red-orange.

Now you need to select another achromatic color. Do you prefer black or white? After you've selected your preference, turn to the appropriate page to read your personalized relationship tips.

If you prefer black, add this new color to what you chose above to become either a yellow-green-black (see page 30), blue-green-black (see page 54), red-orange-black (see page 94), or a red-purple-black (see page 86). If you prefer white, you could become a yellow-green-white (see page 33), blue-green-white (see page 56), red-orange-white (see page 96), or a red-purple-white (see page 88).

WORK TIPS

Appreciate the power you have, and stay on the lookout for what you and those around you need to be successful. You must feel that what you do somehow provides supportive structures or tools for others. Hands-on professions in the medical field, such as nursing or surgery, or in the human-resources field, such as teaching or managing, will help you to better understand yourself.

THINGS WILL BE JUST FINE IF . . .

. . . you put aside your concerns about life and just appreciate your accomplishments. Your new self-awareness will strengthen your belief in yourself. You will see how valuable you are to the world.

CHAPTER ELEVEN

Red and Purple

The Synthesizers

HOW YOU SEE YOURSELF

You enjoy integrating the factual and emotional aspects of situations. After something has occurred, you analyze the event, cut out the nonsense, and pull people together to make things work better. Others see your need for order as somewhat formal. You are at your best when you allow yourself to give advice or be direct. Being supportive makes you feel complete.

Your body language attracts people. Your curiosity generates action. You are sexy. New things may excite and regenerate you, but they can also distract you from finishing what you need to do. Don't procrastinate; finish things before your passion dwindles.

You have a need to know that situations and people are what they seem to be. This characteristic is especially evident when you're in a bad mood. You become very controlling of your environment. You see only the negative at such times. You become so skeptical and overanalytical that everyone's mood is spoiled. You need to synthesize feelings and actions into a workable plan. Otherwise, directing your future will feel like a hardship.

If you like red more than purple, you're more interested in making things work than you are in winning popularity contests. However, you may tend to speak before you consider the consequences of what you say.

If you like purple more than red, you're more concerned about people's reactions. You use your charm and guile to get what you want done.

YOUR ENERGY TYPE: HOW OTHERS SEE YOU

Now that you have read the "How You See Yourself" section, add your favorite achromatic selection (black, white, or brown) to your primary and secondary color choices to determine your energy type and understand how others see you.

> Read your energy-type profile with a friend.
> Many times your friend's comments will give you a
> clearer view of yourself. Keep in mind we are not
> necessarily who we think we are.

Red, Purple, and Black: The Entertainers

DISCOVER YOURSELF

By paying close attention to everyone's emotions, you better understand yourself and others. Your exciting, concerned energy compels people to express themselves. When you hear how others feel, you clearly see their kindness, love, pain, and fear. Your empathy makes them feel important. You captivate them by giving them all your attention. Aren't these the qualities of an ultimate entertainer?

You help people pull their lives together. You are easily spotted at a party: Someone is always pouring his or her heart out to you. Your love of discussing matters of the heart fuels your own desires.

DIVE IN

Use your inexhaustible energy supply to make life an adventure for everyone. Show others how to start things over despite obstacles. Even when things are truly bad, you are able to regenerate and spice things up. Teach others not to be afraid to start something new or reinvent themselves. Tell them about your many experiences. When you're in charge and feeling good about your future, you are an inspiration to everyone.

BUT BEWARE

Outside interference can make it difficult to engage completely in your thought processes. This can destroy your ability to prioritize. Do not let others' opinions make you feel less powerful. They just don't have your ability to assess all the issues. Request the autonomy and time to finish your projects and investigations.

RELATIONSHIP TIPS

You are sexy and seductive. You get what you want. But when love comes to an end, you know it and move on. You don't look back.

If you choose yellow as your least favorite primary color, you are focused on your love life. Problems occur when you get carried away with supporting the other person and he or she does not appreciate or respect you. Then there's hell to pay. Taking you for granted is a big mistake. You can hold a grudge. But staying angry wastes your valuable time and turns other people off. Find your happiness elsewhere.

If you choose blue as your least favorite primary color, you're aware of the many aspects that can cause a relationship to succeed or fail. Your ability to judge people accurately after a first meeting impresses others and is your great talent. However, you can get into trouble if you become distracted by too many thoughts and too much information.

WORK TIPS

You function best in a work environment in which you're in control of all the resources you need and you're in a position to motivate others. You have the power to calm those around you by being quick with solutions and not issuing blame. You think of ways to get things done behind the scenes.

You understand the importance of listening to others' concerns. You are a great team builder. Jobs in nursing, recruiting, politics, religion, or entertainment will give you a sense of fulfillment. You might even consider being a convention or event planner, an administrative assistant, or running a business for which you can set all the terms of operation.

THINGS WILL BE JUST FINE IF . . .

. . . you put away your excessive thoughts about people and situations. You will regain a clear understanding of your feelings. When your heart leads, there's no stopping you.

Red, Purple, and White: *The Forecasters*

DISCOVER YOURSELF

You break everything down to its simplest form. Then you critique past events in order to see the future. Others are amazed at your predictions. You are a soothsayer. With your precautionary warnings, you make sure everything is considered. Others mistake your ability to interpret the facts as intuitive thinking.

DIVE IN

You use common sense to its highest degree. Your insight creates new opportunities. You make sure that your message is heard and tell everyone the consequences they will suffer if they do not address their unrealistic expectations. Your respect for facts keeps you and others well grounded.

As long as you are not too close to a situation or a person, you are almost always right. You have the power to show people where they need to be spending their time and energy.

BUT BEWARE

Your critical skills can limit your future and destroy your best ideas, opportunities, or passions. Too much analysis of everything can make you scattered. You can become extreme in your relationships and endeavors.

So be direct with yourself. It will give you faith and courage to maintain a stronger focus on your objectives. You will be better able to manage the direction of your future.

RELATIONSHIP TIPS

Your appearance and the way you dress are very together. Others will wonder where the chaos hides in you. You are wary of others until you really get to know them. The unknown arouses you. It may be frightening, but that's where the fun is.

If you choose yellow as your least favorite primary color, you have an accurate idea of how to get the exact type of relationship you want. You can also assist others by sharing your relationship knowledge. When you do not give yourself the time to develop a good relationship, you can suddenly find yourself involved in one that you were trying to avoid.

If you choose blue as your least favorite primary color, you see each item that will or will not work when you first meet someone. In your relationships, you can appear to be a bit ditzy at times. In reality, you are just trying to keep things fun and casual. This behavior is mainly a result of your fear of commitment. Sometimes you are so worried about repeating past mistakes that you look for faults in people, and no one measures up to your standards.

WORK TIPS

You have the ability to get the job done right the first time. You are at your best when you are advising the people in power. Expending a great deal of energy on each activity ensures your success.

You know what is needed to complete a task. This allows you to cut out unnecessary steps and not waste time. You will enjoy working with data, making predictions about the future, or analyzing exactly what is real or applicable to each situation.

THINGS WILL BE JUST FINE IF . . .

. . . you stop bombarding yourself with information about everyone and everything around you. You will regain yourself.

Red, Purple, and Brown: The Generators

DISCOVER YOURSELF

Your concerned awareness about the world around you gets attention wherever you go. Others see you as a curious character who needs to know about everything. You constantly attract opportunities. New people and situations stimulate you. You have the power to spice up others' lives. They boost your spirit and give you new perspectives that help you learn and grow.

DIVE IN

Look around. See what looks good, then duplicate it for yourself. Make practical decisions on behalf of other people. Use your natural talents to pinpoint what they can do, even when they're drifting and clueless. Show people how to come to grips with the reality of their circumstances. You'll be able to create bold new solutions to problems.

BUT BEWARE

Your great schemes and desires can cloud your judgment and keep you from accomplishing what you really need to do. One moment you must have something; the next moment you are unsure. Are you making situations or relationships too exciting? When your life feels too intense, slow down and rethink things so that you don't end up spinning your wheels.

RELATIONSHIP TIPS

To understand your energy in a relationship, you need to select another achromatic color. Do you prefer black or white? After you've selected your preference, turn to the appropriate page to read your personalized relationship tips.

If you prefer black, you're a red-purple-black (see page 86). If you prefer white, you're a red-purple-white (see page 88).

WORK TIPS

Focus on careers in which you can analyze your environment, see what looks promising, and then pursue it. It's easy for you to define yourself by what you do. You're a natural at jobs in which you can generate enthusiasm for a product or design a better way of doing something. You can use talents and resources in ways that eclipse conventional practices and expectations.

THINGS WILL BE JUST FINE IF . . .

. . . you know what you want before you expend your energy to acquire it.

Red and Orange

The Humanitarians

HOW YOU SEE YOURSELF

You honor individuality. You believe in walking your own path and speaking your own mind without apologies. If someone gets out of line, you're not about to keep quiet. You're looking for unconditional love, and hope to create an environment where people can express themselves without fear of embarrassment.

You prefer the intimate company of the people you're close to. Big is not necessarily better for you. Small towns, small companies, and small groups of friends hold greater rewards. They allow you to feel worthwhile. Otherwise, too many concerns, environments, friends, or even emotions can eliminate your ability to see the truth.

You perceive what is not working for others. Then, ready or not, you tell them about it. This can frighten away those who don't feel secure in themselves. Others see you as loyal and protective.

Your action-oriented personality hides your sensitive side. This is a defense mechanism. Open up. Show some vulnerability. Like a magnet, you will attract the love and respect you deserve.

If you like red more than orange, you're more preoccupied with your ability to make positive changes in the world than you are with your relationships.

If you like orange more than red, you're more apt to be a facilitator and fix things for the common good.

YOUR ENERGY TYPE: HOW OTHERS SEE YOU

Now that you have read the "How You See Yourself" section, add your favorite achromatic selection (black, white, or brown) to your primary and secondary color choices to determine your energy type and understand how others see you.

> Read your energy-type profile with a friend. Many times your friend's comments will give you a clearer view of yourself. Keep in mind we are not necessarily who we think we are.

Red, Orange, and Black: The Consultants

DISCOVER YOURSELF

The journey to discover your inner self has you reminiscing over your past experiences. You are not afraid to contemplate what did not work and to seek new answers. Evaluating the past helps you better understand what will be of value to you in the future. Those who know you, trust you. They find you endearing.

DIVE IN

You're the one who people expect to get the ball rolling. This is your knack, so use it fully. Enjoy other people's appreciation of you, but don't think anyone else will be able to do for you what you've done for them. Reciprocation isn't what you're really looking for. Being in control, getting things done—this is satisfaction enough. So look for situations in which you can lend a hand.

BUT BEWARE

Avoid sentimentality, and don't concentrate too much on the past. When you examine your emotions over and over, it is difficult for you to be objective. You lose sight of what you need, or forget those who care most about you. Without a strong sense of devotion, you'll soon find yourself spiritually bankrupt. Let other people chase after their fantasies. You need to take care of your own business.

Give yourself the space to reappraise what you have now. Go for long walks or take an extended vacation by yourself. Distance will give you a new perspective. Once you get too close to something, it's hard for you to discern what or who is contributing to your growth.

RELATIONSHIP TIPS

When you know what you want, you aggressively go for it. Friends will see you as personable yet guarded. You are just afraid of being hurt.

If you choose yellow as your least favorite primary color, you are devoted. Problems occur when you get carried away with supporting other people. You lose your ability to know what is best for you. Your relationships can suffer. When you are upset, you seem to disappear. Are you questioning whether those you care about also care about you?

If you choose blue as your least favorite primary color, you find change particularly painful. You're afraid to commit to someone new or change the way you feel. You prefer to stick with the familiar, even though you know things aren't working. Confront these feelings, and a genuine peace will follow.

WORK TIPS

Your loyalty and commitment create a powerful bond with people and form your key to success. Your sharp eye can see what's working; nothing can escape your penetrating gaze. You're a perfectionist. Who you work for means everything to you. You need to feel needed. You sacrifice your personal demands for the good of the company.

Jobs in which others can benefit from your support, such as medicine, child care, or selling a product or service, are best for you.

THINGS WILL BE JUST FINE IF . . .

. . . you let things happen spontaneously. This will create more magic in your life. Don't worry about losing control. Your life will become more about the present instead of a repeat of your past.

Red, Orange, and White: The Resource Directors

DISCOVER YOURSELF

You're all about setting priorities and maximizing the benefits you can receive from the things in your life. You may appear direct and focused on the issues at hand, but you're also deeply interested in the underlying dynamics of different relationships. You motivate people to take a closer look at their lives.

DIVE IN

You realize that success lies in the details. You know how to take a good idea and make it into a great one. But your strength goes even further than that. Aim big. Create new options and better ways of using what you already have. Use your power of connecting resources to expand little ponds into big ones.

BUT BEWARE

You play games with your feelings—often denying them. But feelings can't be turned into facts and vice versa. Make sure that what you have treasured in the past is not left behind. Don't become confused by new opportunities. New doesn't always mean better. Focus, or your heart will become empty.

RELATIONSHIP TIPS

You're a vivacious lover. Meeting new people is a turn-on. But don't become a victim of excesses. In the end, your great need for intimacy will determine your happiness.

If you choose yellow as your least favorite primary color, you are on a journey to better understand how you feel. You are forever creating situations that seem to excite your emotions. Aren't you just creating drama to lose yourself? Don't lose sight of your own happiness. Slow down, and others will see the genuine, lovable you.

If you choose blue as your least favorite primary color, you have a great need to be dedicated to someone. You can hide these feelings from others and sometimes even from yourself. Are you avoiding your heart? Accept that emotions aren't dictated by logic. They'll always disrupt your life. And that's a good thing. Make a commitment to show your feelings. Others will see you as a teddy bear.

WORK TIPS

Choose work environments that allow you some freedom. This latitude will increase your focus and productivity and enable those in charge to recognize exactly what you can accomplish. Their appreciation of your work will build your self-confidence. You'll be able to regenerate and become more powerful.

Show others better ways of using things. A few jobs you might be good at are career counseling, child care, patent law, or computer technology.

THINGS WILL BE JUST FINE IF . .

. . . you allow others to see your emotional side. They'll be able to appreciate fully all the concerns you have and give you the attention that you need.

Red, Orange, and Brown: The Inspectors

DISCOVER YOURSELF

You are very objective. Without any second-guessing, you know exactly what needs to be done and you know from whom to request help. Like Sherlock Holmes, you are consistently discovering clues that help facilitate a resolution. You energize people by improving their lives.

Your dedication to others keeps you moving forward,

especially when you're defending the underdogs. When you fight for their causes, you are also working for your right to be appreciated. After all, every person has the right to be respected for what she does.

DIVE IN

Take advantage of your directness. It eliminates nonsense and misconceptions. You are more concerned about what's actually going on than about people's interpretations. This is what makes you such a great inspector. Nothing can escape your sharp gaze.

Your concerns have healing power. You give of yourself, expecting nothing back other than honest appreciation. Express yourself by giving others physical assistance or emotional reassurance. In doing this, you'll strengthen your own spirit.

BUT BEWARE

You are sometimes so worried about situations going wrong that you don't appreciate what's going right. At times, your critical nature can overshadow the people you care about the most or hinder the completion of a task that is vital to your success. Slow down and contemplate the possibilities in your future. You will pick up speed later at an even more exciting pace.

RELATIONSHIP TIPS

To understand your energy in a relationship, you need to select another achromatic color. Do you prefer black or white? After you've selected your preference, turn to the appropriate page to read your personalized relationship tips.

If you prefer black, you're a red-orange-black (see page 94); if you prefer white, you're a red-orange-white (see page 96).

WORK TIPS

Use your awareness of things and events to fix problems. Your natural talent to fit things together will let you know instantly what will and will not be a success. When working with people, you know what they want to do.

Consider jobs that let you do things by yourself. Creating workable environments will give you great joy and make you feel appreciated for what you do. Concentrate on showing your caring side. Do not allow your defensiveness to cloud your judgment.

THINGS WILL BE JUST FINE IF . . .

. . . you free your mind from obligations. Goodness knows you have a lot of them! You'll obtain a clearer understanding of your needs without being influenced by other people.

Part Three

Learning Your Self-Truth
to Uncomplicate
Your Life

CHAPTER THIRTEEN

Primaries

Your Basic Motivators

What you are speaks so loudly that
I cannot hear what you're saying. . . .
—RALPH WALDO EMERSON

Yellow, blue, and red are the main sources of your energy—the fuel in your engine. The primary colors indicate in the broadest sense who you are. The directness of these strong hues can be energizing or imposing. Before you begin, review your favorite and least favorite primary colors from page 13.

In this chapter you will concentrate on understanding the motivational forces within you. You will be able to tap into your passions and channel them toward making your life more enjoyable and meaningful.

Your favorite primary color determines how you approach life. It indicates what you feel you need to accomplish to be yourself.

Your least favorite primary color, on the other hand, determines what you try to avoid and emotionally suppress. In confronting these concerns you gain the power to stay on track and not let incidental things distract you from your goals.

The primary colors are the source of all other colors. Respecting your favorite and least favorite choices will give you the power to fire up your engine and stay focused on your main objectives in life. Prioritizing your efforts in the rewarding areas of your life will help you maintain your steam and vigor. Obstacles will become insignificant details.

YELLOW FAVORITE

> Knowledge is power.
> —FRANCIS BACON

- ■ *Key words:* realistic, diplomatic, giving
- ■ *Power:* wisdom to know what is needed
- ■ *Motivation:* personal growth

Beyond Words

Finding common ground is the game you play best. You calm troubled situations, bridge differences. Your awareness of others' perspectives enables you to express contrary, unpopular feelings without offending anyone. By keeping people listening, you establish a forum for solutions and possibilities to unfold.

In one-on-one situations you manage to see and understand the other person's point of view. You accept what others need without imposing your own will or agenda on them. You accept people for who they are. You have a knack for keeping the conversation flowing and know precisely where to focus your energy. In groups you keep to yourself; unlike the blues, you retain your energy.

You're a team player and enjoy the supportive role—for example, you'd be happy as the person behind the president. You are flexible. Since you are not a control freak or power hungry, you're able to focus on the task at hand. You deal with the present and don't dwell on the past or obsessively plan for the future. You tend to be spiritual and life-supporting.

The Lovable You

You enjoy the simple pleasures in life, and you give this gift in your relationships as well. You are at your best when those around you are not judgmental or impatient. Rigidity turns you off. Others turn you on when they refrain from making a decision until all the facts are presented.

You're very generous, willing to extend yourself without expecting anything in return. However, you find it difficult to receive. You end up feeling less together, as if you should have acquired what you're given yourself. The people closest to you find it hard to do something special for you.

Allow for give and take. You make others feel important in your life when you let them be there for you. It is advisable to show others your weaknesses; otherwise, you'll find yourself surrounded by people who take advantage of you.

Setting Priorities

Your ability to understand everyone else's point of view is a very powerful tool in the workplace. Knowing how to approach a potential client and getting the boss to listen to a new idea are among your natural talents. Unlike the reds, you are seldom too direct.

You have the power to establish new relationships and move up the corporate ladder. People feel they know where they stand with you, and they are willing to let you help them. You are happy when you're able to give of yourself.

For you, success means growing and learning. You're not overly concerned with money. You would much rather be in a position that gives you a good feeling about yourself than work at a better-paying job you hate. Be careful. You can become too absorbed with the different facets of projects. Constantly remind yourself of the larger picture.

Do It Right

You have the power to take in the beauty that surrounds you and really appreciate everything that life has to offer. Being an integral part of the world is the source of all your energy. You achieve personal growth and enjoy the process of living when absorbed in a task. You are at your best when shopping, relaxing, or encouraging others to hear all the facts before they stop listening.

Don't Go There

When you do things for others to avoid dealing with your own needs, you don't give yourself the time or the energy to think about your own dilemmas. The more upset you become, the more you immerse yourself in the concerns of others. In turn, you become overly docile and unable to help yourself. Your problems, of course, will not go away until you confront them.

Create Passion

Discover those places that allow your fluid, easygoing charm to resonate with people. Avoid overly structured, repressive environments.

YELLOW LEAST FAVORITE: YOU ARE VERY DETERMINED

When you really want something, others had better get out of your way. Your sense of responsibility and urgency keeps those around you moving forward. You create a sense of purpose. You are constantly thinking, *I must do this or that.* Your mind is one step ahead of everyone else's. You are goal-oriented. This gives you the power to persuade those around you to believe in your way of doing things. After all, you look as if you know what you want, even when you're not sure.

The friends and lovers in your life sometimes take a backseat to whatever project you're involved with. But once you meet someone you're really interested in, you obsess over him or her. You want it all and you want it now. Don't be so forceful. Accept people for who they are, not who you want them to be. If you stop trying to change people, they will be better able to reciprocate the love you give.

At work, you are exceptionally focused on results and have a clear idea of the objective at hand. If things take too long, you become impatient. You have a constant need to complete something.

Your first thought is *Why isn't this finished already?* When your sense of urgency is overwhelming, you can send out destructive messages. Others can see you as a person who cares only about the bottom line and not about people. You can end up doing things twice because you are sometimes in too much of a rush.

Slow down; enjoy the process of living. Before you start something new, take the time to appreciate the important things you have already accomplished. You will feel more connected to the world and less isolated. Achieving things is not the only measure of success. Recognize that learning something is reason enough to feel good about yourself.

BLUE FAVORITE

> I dream my painting and then paint my dream.
> —VINCENT VAN GOGH

- **Key words:** planner, initiator, visionary
- **Power:** ability to visualize the future
- **Motivation:** to justify your existence

Beyond Words

You are a dreamer and a visionary—wistful, imaginative, and eccentric. You're preoccupied with the future. Your dreams give you the mental discipline to concentrate and stay on track. You need to justify your life by making a positive impact on the world, even on those you don't know.

Thinking about the future energizes you. Putting forth your ideas and reshaping the world are key to your happiness. You are seeking a more cohesive world. Making sure that everyone is on the same page is a major concern. You need agreement to initiate positive change.

You require recognition. The most idealistic of all the colors, you are often distracted by your own schemes. Mood swings have you feeling downcast one day and euphoric the next. Too much validation from others can make you conceited. Too little can make you depressed.

The Lovable You

You see the sunny side of each person. Putting others on a pedestal makes you feel good about yourself. But be careful. It's vital that your judgment be realistic. Growth in relationships can only be achieved when you perceive things clearly and entirely. Learn to view the negative in conjunction with the positive. Every person has both.

When you first meet someone, appearance is everything. Don't be naive. If you assume that people are who they say they are, you can be vulnerable to con artists. Make sure you appraise people by their actions, not by their words. This will keep you from getting burned. You are especially susceptible to flattery. If you feel someone needs to change or you are repeatedly being burned, be cautious. Set boundaries that protect you. Keep your power. Don't allow someone to get too close until you see beyond appearances.

Setting Priorities

Your ability to visualize helps you be proactive. Blues can fix things before they are broken! When you enjoy your work, you become tenacious about achieving your objective.

This sends the message to those around you that you are in total control. You can pull together a team. Isn't that the formula for a successful beginning?

You need to work for a company where you are appreciated. When you are admired for your contributions, you believe in yourself. You gain the confidence to see the big picture of what the company needs or to develop something original.

Changes in your goals can create an identity crisis. You can become so attached to your goals that you ignore good advice from others. Question those that disagree. Ask them about their concerns. Loosen up. The end result will be even better than you originally envisioned.

Do It Right

When you focus on achieving your dreams, your ideas become so clear in your mind that you can easily see them happening. This gives you the knowledge to be successful and the confidence to believe in your goals. Others can assume you will succeed, even when you aren't sure what to do. You have the power to create images of a bright future for yourself and others.

Don't Go There

You tend to be too rigid and see things as right or wrong, this way or that. Your need to justify why someone disagrees with you makes it hard for you to see other people's perspectives. Reality won't live up to your expectations. Get with it. Allow others to exist as they are without any need to include or exclude them. Otherwise, your false perceptions will continue to make your life difficult. Others can see you as esoteric, even weird, if you become too preoccupied with your thoughts.

Create Passion

Accept others and situations as they are, even when they're not what you expected. You will become content with yourself and better able to create a successful future.

BLUE LEAST FAVORITE: YOU ARE A FAIR CRITIC

You see different ways of deciphering situations, even when it is not acceptable to do so. You know how to categorize and identify what's most helpful. Since you're such a fair critic, you're a natural at setting standards and judging people and performances. Your talent lies in assessing the contributions of others.

You often model yourself after someone you admire and maintain a sharp lookout for a new guru or a new concept that you can dive into completely. When you become truly enthusiastic, you tend to lose yourself in your interests. You become the characters in the book you're reading or those on your favorite television show. Since you often adopt new ideas and behaviors, sometimes you appear trendy.

Strong commitments are difficult for you. It's a real task "getting you to the altar." You find it difficult to put your faith in something that you can't clearly see. Your friends and lovers are often similar to you. They make you feel more together. Dressing like them, or making sure they dress a certain way, can also be a way of feeling closer to them. At times, however, you make others feel rejected because they are different from you.

At work, your attention to detail allows you to juggle many tasks. However, your tendency to critically examine information can be interpreted to mean that you're not supporting the main objective or that you're not on the team. Don't appear so disconnected.

You talk to yourself a lot in an attempt to integrate your rational and emotional sides. Respect both aspects of your personality. There's room for compromise. Stay focused on your main objective, and don't get distracted by other issues. Your increased mental discipline will help you see the big picture, and you'll be better able to plan your future.

RED FAVORITE

> Do what you can, with what you have, where you are.
> —THEODORE ROOSEVELT

- *Key words:* practical, resourceful, direct
- *Power:* ability to use lessons from experience to improve things
- *Motivation:* to better control your world

Beyond Words

You know exactly what you want. Money, power, and status give you a sense of security, but ultimately you use them as a means of expression. This is your primary goal. You're not one to hoard your wealth. On the contrary, you would give the shirt off your back for those you're concerned about.

You are ambitious, driven, confident, and outgoing. Red is a demanding, controlling color. It's also a practical color. You don't want to remake the world in your own image, as the blues do. You just want to be in charge of fixing things. You have little tolerance for inefficiencies.

Even though your expressive style can make you appear extravagant, you are conservative. You learn what you need from past experiences. You are more realistic than someone who likes blue, because you have less need for validation and have a stronger sense of your own worth.

The Lovable You

You know exactly who you are and what you want. You believe that you do not exist until you express yourself, and it is common for you to state your opinions boldly. You feel complete when you're clear about where you stand. Your concern for the key people in your life gives you the power to focus on what you need to do.

You need physical contact to feel worthwhile. When you're having fun, you act like a fourteen-year-old. You make lots of noise and talk about what others are doing. This is especially true with friends who also like red. You tell stories about your experiences.

When you are comfortable in your environment, you're so outgoing and confident that everyone knows you exist. If you are a woman, however, you can be viewed as too strong. Since in many cultures women are judged by the way they enter a conversation, your vivacity can be seen as too direct, or as unacceptable behavior for a female. So if you are a

woman who likes red, be aware of what is and is not considered acceptable. Then choose your direction and express
yourself tactfully. It's okay if some men see you as difficult.
Just make sure that the man you commit to accepts you for
who you are. Otherwise, his ego can hinder you from expressing yourself, or you may run him off with your bossiness.

Setting Priorities

Your practical approach allows you to evaluate things and the
people around you. You perform best when you are acting in
the best interest of others. Your thinking is consistent and very
fact-based. You help others around you to recognize the reality
of a situation, and you let them know when they are not being
practical. Your opinions and observations correct their focus.
You are motivated by the opportunity to direct others.

Money is important to you. You need to know if
you're going to get your share. After all, money can be a
means of acknowledging a job well done, and it shows that
you are important to your employer. The accumulation of
resources is your way of proving your self-worth. You
believe strongly in getting it right the first time and are irri-
tated when others leave promises unfulfilled. You have little
patience with attitudes that reflect laziness or unwillingness
to work. You believe rewards must be earned. If this atti-
tude is carried too far, you can earn a reputation as a hard
taskmaster. Others may see you as a perfectionist.

Do It Right

Express yourself with sharp exuberance. You make things
work better when you hold nothing back. Let your ideas

and plans land with a big bang. You are at your best when shaking things up and getting things to work right. When others recognize that you have clear motives and expectations, they respect you or those you are protecting.

Don't Go There

You can be too direct and seek too much control of those around you. Others can see you as too conservative, limited, overly concerned with what has worked before and unwilling to look at what might work better. You become negative, too literal, and expect people to be as consistent and rational as you are. This can create an environment where positive change is difficult. At your worst, you are tyrannical. Too much power can corrupt you. You can lose sight of other people and be done in by your ego.

Create Passion

Temper your need to constantly evaluate situations and others' actions. You will see in detail what is working for you.

RED LEAST FAVORITE:
WHEN YOU SPEAK, OTHERS LISTEN

You analyze your thoughts before you speak. This gives you the ability to articulate in great depth how you feel. Therefore, when you speak, others listen. You can be impulsive. All of a sudden you could be doing something you never imagined you'd do. This behavior sometimes results in stories about you that you would not divulge to anyone.

Your impulsive actions are manifestations of suppressed feelings and desires.

You are the confidant. Others trust you with their greatest secrets. You make them feel important to you. In fact, many times you hear more than you want to hear. When someone is telling you something that makes you feel uncomfortable, your face doesn't show a negative expression, even though you're thinking, *Help! Why are you telling me this?* Therefore, they keep on talking. You hear details and stories that make soap operas sound boring.

With your friends and lovers, your hidden feelings create mystery. They make you sexy. Your curiosity has a magnetic effect that attracts the vulnerable part of others. After a relationship has started, the other person can become frustrated if you do not tell him or her what you need. As a child, did you feel that if you expressed how you felt, one or both of your parents wouldn't approve of you? Is your hesitation related to that fear? You must believe that when you express your needs to those who care about you, they will care even more.

At work, you occasionally forget to define what activities need to be done. This can make you a poor manager. Be firm. State each task, duty, or expectation in detail so that your coworkers know specifically what you want. Write things down, then follow up.

When you don't initially speak up, others might see you as wimpy, weak, or politically neutral. Simply tell them, without emotion, "You will hear from me when I'm ready." They will then see that you have the tactical skills to say the appropriate things at the right time. This discovery will increase their respect for you.

WHERE DO YOU FIT IN?

Combine your favorite and least favorite primary color selections to see the overall motivating power within you.

Yellow Favorite, Red Least Favorite

You're the original "people person" with a flair for the social scene. A natural at public relations, you have the knack to see the other person's point of view without being judgmental. For that reason alone, people are willing to trust and confide in you. This provides you with the unvarnished facts needed to make decisions. Don't allow your support for others to interfere with your own future.

Yellow Favorite, Blue Least Favorite

What some people and companies wouldn't give for you! You possess the uncanny ability to quickly grasp what those around you need. You can often locate the missing ingredient and turn what might have been a failure into a rousing success. Remain constantly aware of the big picture, and don't get bogged down by any one task.

Blue Favorite, Yellow Least Favorite

You are a wonderful strategist, able to plan future designs with a clear, sharp, and imaginative style. You love fantasy. However, while you may engage a plan with enthusiasm, what you think you want often differs from what you really need. Be more pragmatic, more sensible. Recognize that this isn't a perfect world. The faster you develop more realistic expectations, the more successful you will be.

Blue Favorite, Red Least Favorite

You see the possibilities and limitations of your goals. This is a gift. You do not get angry if your future differs markedly from the way you envision it. You steadfastly hold on to your vision of where you want to go. Be mindful to clearly communicate all your expectations and wishes, or you may find that you don't have the respect or support you need.

Red Favorite, Yellow Least Favorite

You are a perfectionist. More important, you know how to fix what isn't working. However, when overburdened, you have a tendency to see only the details or else skip the details entirely. Others may regard you as rigid. Give yourself the chance to step back and reappraise things. There are many ways besides yours to accomplish a task.

Red Favorite, Blue Least Favorite

You have the enviable talent of being able to appraise situations far better than those around you can. Your ability to categorize things and estimate their value, however, can be lost in the specifics of a task. Staying focused on your overall objective will go a long way toward making you more successful. Don't let your concentration on the details sweep away your future.

YOU AND I

If your friend, partner, or coworker selected . . .

The same favorite primary color as you did, he or she gives you the confidence to believe in yourself. He or she will motivate you.

A different favorite primary color than you did, he or she enables you to see new possibilities and teaches you how to be more productive.

A Yellow with a Yellow

You allow each other to see your powers of flexibility. You create a world where conversations flow about the pleasant things in life. Your relationship is like a melody. Together you effortlessly attract others who give both of you new sources of stimulation. When you disagree, you simply change the subject. If this process is allowed to continue, your relationship is weakened.

A Blue with a Blue

You stay focused on the future. You talk about your plans. You see each other's wishes as if they were a reality. You encourage each other to "just do it." When you disagree, at first there is little to talk about. Both of you become stubborn. You both believe you are right. However, after your initial clash you usually compromise because both of you are uncomfortable with too much interpersonal conflict.

A Red with a Red

You constantly inspect things. You like to talk about everyone else. Marriages, dates, divorces, and sex are big topics. You want to hear about how others are living their lives. You both want to know all the details. You guessed it! You two love gossip. It gives you new perspectives on how to live your own lives. If one of you dwells on his or her dilemma, the other will take over and become bossy. Then all hell breaks loose.

A Yellow with a Blue

You help each other stay focused on your relationship. As a yellow, you tell the blue when she is losing touch with reality by thinking in a too linear way. As a blue, you tell the yellow how to better determine where his relationship or circumstance is going. Together you're able to balance perspectives and ideas, keeping them relevant.

As a yellow, you teach blue how to understand different perspectives and to enjoy life. You teach her the art of flexibility. You also open the blue's world to new resources. By helping her to be more realistic about her expectations, you enable blue to feel more like a winner. In a crisis you perceive blue as paying too much attention to her dreams, instead of to reality.

As a blue, you help the yellow better define his future. You turn his factual perspective into a structured plan. You admire the yellow's flexibility, yet become frustrated when you feel that goals aren't being met. You can see his flexibility as a sign of weakness or a lack of direction. The yellow then clashes with your authoritarianism. He feels that you are jumping to conclusions too quickly instead of considering all the information available.

A Yellow with a Red

You can clearly define situations. As a yellow, you put a quick end to the red's love of gossip. As a red, you keep the yellow focused on how to accomplish her goals. This helps the yellow become more reliable.

As a yellow, you enable red to see the limitations of his rules and agendas. You make him more flexible and better able to enjoy what he has and whom he is with. Red can then relax and feel less confined. In a crisis, you see red as too negative and overly structured.

As a red, you teach yellow how to be more specific and targeted in performance. The yellow loves your eye for detail. Too many rules, however, make the yellow feel confined. In a crisis, you fuel the yellow's frustrations by bossing her around and failing to listen to her point of view.

A Blue with a Red

You can accomplish any task. As a blue, you help the red believe that things can be better. Your dreams can make the red's tedious, task-oriented day go away. On the other hand, as a red, your eye for detail teaches the blue how to make things work. With your "chop, chop, chop," you cut out what's not necessary. You make blue's ideas work.

As a blue, you constantly entertain the red with your ideas. You encourage the more task-oriented red to dream. By showing the red how to be less concerned with details, you open the red's eyes. You make looking forward to the future more fun. In a crisis, your ego may be wounded. You then discount the contributions of the red, dismissing her input as negative and nonconstructive.

As a red, you force the blue to express his needs more clearly. You coach him on how to pinpoint what he wants so that he can accomplish the realization of his ideas. By forcing the blue to face limitations, you help him to recognize that reworking is a normal part of life. When the blue ignores your input, you lose respect for his creative contribution. You see him as incompetent, unaware of important details necessary to complete any creative endeavor.

YOUR PRIMARY FOCUS

If you like two primary colors equally, you can become confused about what to do next. You are pushing yourself to be more than you are right now. Others will see this pushy side of you as hard to understand. It's simply your way to gain clarity on what you want.

If you prefer the colors in the primary category overall, you are in good company. Very high-profile individuals and royalty who were evaluated preferred the primary category as well. Your formal composure will also make you appear to be a prince, princess, or a commander-in-chief. Avoid dwelling on serious concerns all the time and reveal your vulnerability, or you will feel alone.

If you did not prefer the colors in this category overall, you are going through a career crisis or avoiding doing what you really want to do. You might find the brightness of these colors a bit imposing. Be more directed in your life. Recognize the consequences you are incurring by not being more specific about what you need to do.

Laughing Out Loud

You will find yourself attracted to people who dislike the primary color you prefer. Your favorite selection will be the same as their least favorite. They naturally demonstrate the qualities you are striving to achieve. Sometimes, though, they really agitate the weakest, most uncomfortable aspects of your personality.

Those who prefer the same primary color as you do confirm your sense of identity. They restore your faith in yourself. However, they can also be embarrassingly upsetting to you. Because they are so much like you, they also force you to see exactly who you are not. If you are really like one of your parents, or if one of your children is like you, you know this feeling well.

Let me share with you my favorite color, blue. When I talk with people who dislike blue, I discover that their point of view is distinctly different from mine. Their questions force me to confront what I am most afraid to see. At times, I have even rejected their valuable perspective only to find out later that they were right on.

THE LANGUAGE OF PRIMARY COLORS

Yellow Is Absorbing Knowledge

Yellow is the lightest color in the spectrum. It is a search for a more realistic perspective that will create hope and a brighter tomorrow. Likewise, people who prefer yellow have the ability to study situations and relationships without a preconceived mind-set. Yellows are concerned with understanding the world around them.

Blue Is Being Cohesive

Blue is the coldest color in our atmosphere. Likewise, people who prefer blue are able to deny the natural warmth and energy of the present to anticipate the future. Like water, which forms a cohesive chemical bond, those who prefer blue pull together different entities to form a cohesive focus. Blue is future-based thoughts. It's about initiating dreams.

Red Is Directing

Red directs physical change. Whether it is the molten lava inside the center of the earth, a fire burning in a forest, or bacteria acting on an organism, red is the agent of change. Likewise, people who prefer red are constantly improving on the status quo. Red is about directing resources.

When Your Primary Colors Change

Generally speaking, your favorite primary color does not change after your early twenties. If you are questioning your life goals, it can change until you become more comfortable with yourself. Your least favorite primary color is the last to change. If it changes, you're probably in a highly reactive period of your life.

The Primary IQ Quiz

Answer True or False.

Yellow Favorite Primary Color

1. They're threatening in the workplace.　T　　F
2. They're flexible.　T　　F

Yellow Least Favorite Primary Color

3. They rarely have to do things twice.　T　　F
4. They can be real jerks.　T　　F

Blue Favorite Primary Color

5. They live for their dreams.　T　　F
6. They're realistic about ideas.　T　　F

Blue Least Favorite Primary Color

7. They're hungry for marriage.　T　　F
8. They talk to themselves a lot.　T　　F

Red Favorite Primary Color

9. They say what they think.　T　　F
10. They never discuss other people.　T　　F

Red Least Favorite Primary Color

11. They blurt out how they feel.　T　　F
12. They know a lot about everyone.　T　　F

*Answers on the next page

Answers to the Primary IQ Quiz

Yellow Favorite Primary Color

1. F They are about as threatening as a puppy dog.
2. T They are so flexible, they can become your fantasy of the moment.

Yellow Least Favorite Primary Color

3. F Their faster-than-a-speeding-bullet personality can really blow it the first time.
4. T If they know what they want, you better get out of their way.

Blue Favorite Primary Color

5. T Just ask about them, and get ready for an earful.
6. F Is there ice water in hell?

Blue Least Favorite Primary Color

7. F The idea of walking down the aisle makes them shake.
8. T They're their own best friend.

Red Favorite Primary Color

9. T Like Madonna or Oprah Winfrey.
10. F Only if their jaws are wired shut!

Red Least Favorite Primary Color

11. F Not unless they're pushed, tipsy, or ticked off.
12. T Ask them; they probably know lots about you.

CHAPTER FOURTEEN

Secondaries

How You Relate

When the mind is thinking, it is talking to itself.
—Plato

Green, purple, and orange make up the secondary color category. They determine how you reason in your relationships and create bonds in the world around you. The harmonic vibrations of the secondary colors can be soothing or irritating. Green is the child of yellow and blue; purple is the child of blue and red; orange is the child of red and yellow. Before you begin, review your secondary color selections from page 13.

In this chapter, you will learn more about how other people affect your priorities, needs, choices, failures, job performance, and contributions.

Your favorite secondary color reveals your actual thinking process when it comes to your desires, needs, and goals. It shows how you relate to others.

Your least favorite secondary color represents your subliminal needs that are often ignored. It symbolizes your emotional way of confronting your thoughts about what you want from other people.

The secondary colors translate the world around you

into language. They reflect your thinking process. What do you consider first? Last? As you read this chapter, consider the pluses and minuses of the way you prioritize facts and feelings. Simple awareness of your thinking will make you a star.

GREEN FAVORITE

> The purest and most thoughtful minds are those which love colour the most.
>
> —JOHN RUSKIN

- *Key words:* nurturing, concerned, comfortable
- *Power:* creating supportive environments
- *Motivation:* to understand who you are and what you want

Your Thoughts

You're the perfect audience for others when they need to discuss their problems. They interpret your concern as encouragement to talk about their lives. They feel you can see beyond outward appearances and truly understand who they are. Like fertile soil, you nurture people so that their dreams can grow.

You are initially open to the world. In fact, you probably liked most of the colors in the Dewey Color System! You appear innocent, but your curiosity makes you quite knowledgeable. You know about life, either through your own activities or through listening to others.

What Turns You On

You understand people's true intentions. When talking with people you've just met, or with friends or lovers, at first you put their needs before your own. This behavior allows you to walk in their shoes and see how they feel inside. Then, you step back to objectively view their intentions. You see others for who they really are.

You are attracted to someone who is intellectually inspiring. Intelligence is a real turn-on. It entices your curiosity. Even when there's absolutely no physical attraction, you are still able to maintain a friendship. Sometimes this can be confusing to the other person, because your initial attraction can be misinterpreted.

You marry or commit for security. This might mean having a home with children, having lots of money, being cared about, or just having a stabilizing personality in your life. Sometimes the physical or mental characteristics of the person you marry are sufficient to give you this sense of security. Whatever form it takes, the need for security is the key factor in your decision-making.

Your Natural Talents

You are practical and reliable. Everyone appreciates how supportive you are and how you establish a nurturing environment. You're a natural at managing their talents. In fact, you are excellent at managing materials and financial resources.

These qualities allow you to deal with the public. They support your ability to do well in professions that include interviewing, training, counseling, or working with children. You need to work for a company that will be consistent in its employment policies. This will allow you to feel secure about your future.

As you mature, seeking a stable career position will increase in importance. If your practical affairs aren't in order, you cannot be at peace. You need to be disciplined and work hard if you are to acquire material possessions. Some careers that will enhance your passions are banking, investing, insurance, business management, medicine, or consulting.

Your Life's a Party When . . .

. . . you know how others feel and they support and care about you. When people need you, you are there for them. You are good at listening to people and giving them solid advice on how to solve their problems. Your concern for their well-being makes them feel more secure.

Your Hang-Ups Emerge When . . .

. . . you question your identity. You can feel as if you are too close to someone and blame him or her for this dependence. You begin to withdraw and become consumed with yourself instead of being the supportive person you normally are. This can shock or upset those who count on you. The more confident you are, the less this behavior occurs.

Be a Star

Accept your sensitivity as a great gift, not a weakness. It will give you the strength to better support yourself and those around you. Cherish it and you will grow.

GREEN LEAST FAVORITE:
YOU SEEK TO BE NURTURED

You seek to be nurtured by providing for others. You need to believe that your concern for them will make them loyal to you. You will even sacrifice your own happiness. When you feel good, you remember to take care of yourself. When you are down, you have a tendency to avoid your supportive personal routine completely.

Your independent nature allows you to work for long periods of time without asking for help. You feel like an explorer. You go to extremes to make sure that coworkers and customers are happy. You are concerned for them, as if they were your children. You can, in fact, become so busy saving others that you lose yourself. Don't try to fix things until you've heard all the facts of a situation.

When you're upset, you become frustrated and emotionally spent. Only when you hit rock bottom do you realize what you need and tell others exactly what you want. It is as if you expect people to intuitively understand what your needs are. Like a child, you are hoping someone will care enough to notice that you want nurturing, too. When you were growing up, did you believe you had to take on the responsibilities of an adult? Did you have to give support to your brothers or sisters or be there for one of your parents? Now, when you ask for help, do you feel it signifies that you are weak and powerless?

Ask yourself every morning when you first get up, *What do I really need today, and who will support me after I tell them what I want?* Then listen to your feelings. Don't deny what you really want because of your concern for others. Selfishness for you would be a virtue. Everyone around you will be happier when you tell them what you want. The quicker you proclaim it, the better your relationships and life will become.

PURPLE FAVORITE

> To think is to differ.
> —CLARENCE DARROW

- **Key words:** determined, dramatic, empowering
- **Power:** seeing new possibilities, ideas, and strategies
- **Motivation:** to become more self-empowered

Your Thoughts

Your search for personal power is certainly no secret. You are reflective and thoughtful. Others see you as witty, clever, and full of pride, and they are right. You need to show off your stuff. You are strong-willed. You know exactly what you want from others.

To say you can't achieve something is to say that you do not have possibilities in life. Others turn you on when they challenge you. It makes you work even harder. Your sense of drama wins people over. You are a great motivator. Your enthusiasm creates endless possibilities. You see significance in things that others miss. When your goal is defined, you are a leader and people are willing to follow you.

What Turns You On

You are attracted to a person's energy. You don't really know why, you just are. Your decision to get married, though, is based on physical appearances, a special look that catches your eye. You can feel, for example, that someone was just "too cute" to let go. Attraction is difficult for you to deny when that special look is evident.

Relationships mean serious business to you. You're loyal, but wary about forming new bonds. This can sometimes work to your detriment. Instead of experiencing life, you stand back, resisting what you know is right, analyzing yourself as if you were writing a book. You place your needs on a shelf to be dealt with later. Later, however, never comes.

Withdrawing emotionally is how you protect yourself. If you don't play the game, of course, you can't get hurt. All of a sudden you may realize that your friend or lover has become emotionally distant from you or is even gone. In denying yourself what you really needed, you have made him or her feel unimportant to you.

Your Natural Talents

Everyone knows how easily you can come up with new ideas and ways of doing things. You salivate for a mental challenge. This makes you a natural in the business world. To construct something new is a big turn-on. It allows you to see your own potential. You love to be included in the developmental part of a project. In fact, you're going to tell them your idea even if they don't ask.

Your dramatic expression helps motivate those around

you. You encourage the potential in others. Your sharp tongue, however, can get you into lots of trouble, and sometimes people will not hear your message correctly. If your facts are exaggerated, others will lose faith in your information.

Your Life's a Party When . . .

. . . you look into the cause of things and analyze all the possibilities. You're the first to speak up, even when no one else will, and to take a stand against the crowd. Determined? You bet you are! No one stands in your way. You have the ability to do what those around you say you cannot do.

Your Hang-Ups Emerge When . . .

. . . you assume things that have nothing to do with a person's actual behavior. Dwelling on what should be or what could have been can lead to a lot of disappointment. You can become stuck analyzing your past experiences. Why someone did something is not for you to say. This projective thinking can even make you loyal to a person who has not earned the privilege.

Your assumptions can make prioritizing the things you want to do difficult. Be suspicious of yourself when you claim to be too charitable or feel emotionally wounded. You will make life a lot easier for everyone when you declare, rather than justify, your wants. Be especially careful of assuming you have changed. Small efforts are not enough. You must deal with the issues that real change requires.

Be a Star

Wisdom is gained by experiencing life. Constantly assuming what will happen only eliminates possibilities and diminishes your passion. Let each situation unfold on its own.

PURPLE LEAST FAVORITE: YOU ARE LOGICAL

Facts come before feelings. You disregard emotions in order to get a more precise view of the people and situations around you. You clearly see when a relationship is not working and can end it without a lot of wasted energy. You have the talent of knowing what not to believe in. You choose your friends and lovers in a very objective way. You have lifetime friendships. It is almost as if to lose a friend is to lose memories.

In the workplace you are known for being very methodical. This gives you the ability to handle an emotionally charged situation and stay focused. You weigh only the pertinent facts and then set priorities.

When you're upset, you stop communicating. You experience a mental burnout. Suddenly you become confronted with all of your hidden fears. Your deeply buried past feelings may not even be related to current issues. Yet they still remain and can stop you from knowing how you feel in the present. During these crisis moments, your belief in people dwindles. You don't invest in the future or encourage others to believe in themselves.

Sometimes you make it uncomfortable for your loved ones to express themselves to you. This can lead to pent-up resentment, causing them to explode. Since you don't confront yourself with who you aren't, those around you don't either. This creates an information gap. Situations will arise where one moment everything is fine, and the next moment it's a disaster.

You forget things easily because your memory tends to be selective. You do not let your emotions interfere with your reasoning. You have a tendency to forget your dreams. To remember them might make your fear of knowing what is inside you manifest itself.

Your personal potential will only be realized when you allow yourself to be more forgiving of your emotions. Allow them to exist by trying not to rationalize everything.

ORANGE FAVORITE

> A man is judged by what he does, not by what he says.
> —ARISTOTLE

- ■ *Key words:* bold, sentimental, dedicated
- ■ *Power:* implementing change without disruption
- ■ *Motivation:* to discover how things are made

Your Thoughts

You are dedicated to your job, hobbies, friends, and family. Your realistic view of the world allows you to identify what is not important. You are a doer and understand that eggs need to be broken if you want an omelet. You have a sharp eye for spotting physical things that are not working. Since you have the forcefulness of red tempered with the awareness of yellow, you can get things done without ruffling feathers.

You're very sentimental. The older you become, the more you will have a tendency to talk about the past. If you have children and grandchildren, they'll get lots of affection from you. You're the first to show photos. You take pleasure in placing photos of those you love all around the house. You think about those you care about all the time.

You like physical activities. Driving fast cars, playing sports, and repairing things are some of the pastimes you might enjoy. You take pride in what you own and maintain your possessions. You have a bold approach to life.

What Turns You On

Everyone likes you. You're charismatic, lovable, affectionate, and big on hugs. After all, orange is the warmest color in our atmosphere. You are usually a hit at parties. You have a lot of friends. You need to touch others to know what they are made of. Touching gives you the ability to see the truth in situations and relationships. It is your way of letting others know you are listening and care about them. You build relationships with people who can teach you things.

When first meeting someone, you hide the sensitive side of yourself. You are simply afraid to show the vulnerable you. Your defenses are all they see. They can even believe that you are somewhat formal or traditional.

You are lured into a relationship by the way a person looks. Your decision to get married, however, is based on intellect. You dedicate yourself to someone who is smart, and usually marry for life.

Your Natural Talents

You're a very loyal employee who believes in what you do and whom you work for. You're the person who tells everyone how great your company is. When your employer does not return your appreciation by believing in and supporting you, your loyalty is quickly withdrawn. You have the ability to eliminate what is not important to you without expending much energy.

You unemotionally explain the task at hand. Your coworkers respect you for being logical. Even when they disagree with you, they never see you as attacking them or their positions. After all, you're the one who usually has a clear, practical purpose in mind before starting a new project. You work best when there is constant social interaction. It especially turns you on to be needed. Chaos is no problem; you enjoy searching for solutions and doing a difficult task well.

Your Life's A Party When . . .

. . . you are dedicated. By boldly asking questions that others avoid, you figure out how things are made or how situations occurred. This allows you to make changes without disrupting or upsetting the status quo. By acting logically, not emotionally, you help others realize the truth. This is your talent. You make change less painful.

Your Hang-Ups Emerge When . . .

. . . someone is critical of something you have done or should have done. You get defensive. The criticism becomes a personal matter to you, one in which you feel that your dedication is being questioned. Your objectivity goes out the window. Don't make such a fuss. No one is questioning how much you care or how much you do. You care a lot and do more than your share.

Be a Star

Protect yourself by being dedicated to someone who is also dedicated to you. Loyalty to the right person or position makes you feel secure, and you become successful as a result.

ORANGE LEAST FAVORITE: YOU ARE OPEN TO THE WORLD

When you feel good, your naive approach to life can charm even the most jaded. Others see you as a considerate, nice person. When you feel bad, you distrust yourself or blame others. Your world becomes a bitter, lonely place.

When you first meet someone, you are either too serious or not serious enough. There is no middle ground. This may keep you from finding the relationships that you need. Being too serious hides the fun part of you, and being too carefree can make others think that you are not sincere.

At work, you're a natural at keeping customers and coworkers happy. You're concerned, considerate, and hardworking. Pleasing others motivates you. On the downside, your strong desire to please can make you commit to unrealistic deadlines. You can miss the practical realities of how long it takes to accomplish a task. You're then forced to overextend yourself, working so hard you become physically exhausted, even sick. Sure, sometimes you can accomplish a great deal of work, but is it really worth it?

Stop indulging your unrealistic expectations. Before you expect something from others or commit to doing something, ask more questions. You will see people's underlying desires that way. Accept the fact that everyone is doing exactly what he or she wants to do anyway. Aren't you doing what you really need to do as well?

Evaluate your feelings. Make it your goal to eliminate what you do not want to do and who you do not enjoy being with. Only then will you realize what and whom you need.

FINDING YOUR NICHE

The combination of your favorite and least favorite secondary color selections shows how you relate to others.

Green Favorite, Purple Least Favorite

You listen for information, not emotions. Your flawless logic gives you the ability to calm those around you. You give them the power to prioritize the facts, not the feelings. Your dilemma in life is to be more comfortable with your emotions. You discount them before you have a chance to feel them. When you concentrate solely on the literal and factual, you destroy the human experiences you need to learn more about yourself.

Green Favorite, Orange Least Favorite

Since people can read you like an open book, you often listen to their counsel. You can bond one-on-one with another person right away, but you need to learn how to share yourself without losing yourself. One moment you're concerned about your own needs; the next moment you're obsessing about other people. When you have the courage to disassociate from what you expect from yourself to see the truth of a situation, you'll know better who you are.

Purple Favorite, Green Least Favorite

You encourage people to be the best that they can be. Being concerned for them inspires you and gives you new insights into your own power. If you feel you are rehearsing your expressions before you say them, beware. You're requesting something that's more about what you need than what the other person wants to give. Are you expecting to gain more control of a person if you are very nice to him? Don't get so caught up in others' concerns. Accept that your surroundings and how others feel are not about you, and you will learn how powerful you are.

Purple Favorite, Orange Least Favorite

You observe how powerful others can be to better understand your own desires. When you become concerned about other people, you experience their passion. This allows you to better define what you enjoy. Your enthusiasm then unleashes your own passion. It starts new projects. You need to listen to your inner voice, however, for what you expect from others before you set out looking for exciting opportunities. Otherwise, you will become frustrated. Your overly high expectations of people and circumstances can make you mistrustful when things don't turn out right. Then you start to whine about how you've been let down in the past.

Orange Favorite, Purple Least Favorite

You have great concern for others, but sometimes you hide your feelings about people from yourself. You have strong analytical skills and know what is or is not important. At work, this is a helpful quality; at home, it can be a disaster. Your dilemma in life is to make sure that your deeply hidden emotions aren't negated by your logic. Give yourself the opportunity to feel the great love you have inside. Otherwise, you can become bitter and destroy the very core of who you are.

Orange Favorite, Green Least Favorite

Your dedication to your work and those you love is boundless. There is nothing you will not do to make things work better. When you feel that those around you are not supporting you, however, you become very defensive. This defensiveness appears suddenly, because you hide your feelings—even from yourself. Try not to be overly dedicated. It is unhealthy for everyone involved if you completely lose yourself in causes and other people's problems.

GETTING IN SYNC

If your partner, friend, or coworker selected . . .

The same favorite secondary color as you did, he or she helps you to understand the way you think more clearly.

A different favorite secondary color than you, he or she shows you a different way of viewing a situation or person.

A Green with a Green

Together, you create the feeling of being at home. At your best, you give each other a stronger sense of self. You feel as though you are one. To help another green is to help yourself. Both of you create a world that allows the other to better understand who he is. This is a secure place to be, a safe haven. At your worst, you see the other's self-involved quality as evidence that he's not concerned about you.

A Purple with a Purple

You assume many things. At your best, you both can generate new ideas and develop new things. Your wit and sense of drama make life fun and exciting. Others can even believe the two of you are having an argument when they witness your provoking sharp tongues and biting sarcasm, when in fact it's your way of having fun. At your worst, you assume "facts" that are not correct. This can make you both pessimistic and paranoid.

An Orange with an Orange

You reinforce each other's accomplishments. At your best, you create a world where you both feel appreciated. You constantly acknowledge how much the other has contributed to a project. Others see you as sentimental one moment and strictly logical the next. At your worst, you both can become overly critical and constantly examine unimportant things and minor transgressions.

A Green with a Purple

You increase each other's self-awareness and resiliency to transcend failure. As a green, you show a purple how to slow down and enjoy the pleasures of everyday life. In a crisis, you can become self-absorbed and ignore a purple's passion for the relationship.

As a purple, you help a green see empowering possibilities within herself and encourage her to be more self-confident. As a defense, you can become entrenched in what you are doing, and ignore the green.

A Green with an Orange

You make people and things come together. As a green, you reinvigorate an orange by helping him to stop focusing on past failures. The orange then stops being overly sensitive and is better able to contribute to the world.

As an orange, your recognition of past accomplishments helps a green feel proud. But under stress, you can make a green feel forgotten, due to your compulsive dedication to others. You then turn critical, annoyed by the green's need for "constant" attention.

A Purple with an Orange

You create realistic dreams. As a purple, you teach an orange to see the possibilities of the future. In turn, the orange's analytical side makes your expectations more realistic.

As an orange, you become negative when the purple is distracted by grandiose ideas. If you appear too consumed with the affairs of other people or with your job, the purple can feel left out and neglected.

YOUR SECONDARY CONNECTION

If you like two secondary colors equally, you are uncertain about what you want out of a relationship. Others can feel that they know you, and then an entirely different person appears before them. Confusing? You bet you are! No one can please you or even be close to you unless they know what you need.

If you preferred all the colors in the secondary category overall, you are always thinking about others. You can be excessive in your need to be close to someone. This is especially evident in a crisis. You completely lose yourself. Always thinking about others makes it difficult for them to give back to you.

If you find the secondary category colors disconcerting, you are bitter from a past relationship or not available emotionally. To you, these colors are too open to the world. Stop identifying with those sad love songs on the radio! Show your vulnerability by letting your significant other or a possible relationship candidate see your authentic self.

Laughing Out Loud

When I owned a staffing company, I trained hundreds of sales representatives. Most of them preferred purple—just as I do. Driving back from sales calls, we purples would always assume we knew what the clients needed, instead of asking them. It was really scary. Agreement among ourselves somehow made our inferences "facts." Later we would be shocked to find that our "information" was erroneous.

The sales representatives who preferred green had a natural consultant approach. They used their listening skills to build client rapport. Their nurturing yet conclusive approach made each client feel more in charge. Those who preferred purple were amazed that such a low-key approach could make a sale.

I had many oranges who were successful in sales. When they were dedicated, they would go to war, not to work. Hands-on projects allowed them to get really involved with fixing everything. They preferred working on more tangible goals or projects.

THE LANGUAGE OF SECONDARY COLORS

Green Is Nurturing

Green provides the nurturing infrastructure for life. Fertile soil contains the ingredients that allow plants to grow.

Likewise, people who prefer green are nurturing and are aware of the delicate balance that our environment demands. They understand the most basic needs and provide the underpinnings for physical existence.

Purple Is Seeing Possibilities

Purple is the darkest color in the spectrum. Likewise, people who prefer purple are looking to define themselves. They have the courage to look into the darkness of their emotions. A purple is concerned with defining the self in order to become more powerful. They know that personal growth starts with considering the possibilities.

Orange Is Dissecting

Orange is the warmest color in our atmosphere. Heat is the force of change. It transforms matter. Likewise, people who prefer orange have the ability to transform things by analyzing how they were made. As in osmosis, they absorb what is working, but they also eliminate what is not so that something new can grow. An orange is concerned with creating constructive change.

When Your Secondary Colors Change

The degree to which you like your favorite secondary color determines how involved you are in your personal and professional relationships. If it changes, you are going through a tough relationship period. If your least favorite secondary color changes abruptly, you have learned a great lesson about those around you.

The Secondary IQ Quiz

Answer True or False.

Green Favorite Secondary Color

1. They're innocent in both thoughts and actions.   T   F
2. They're turned on by intelligence.   T   F

Green Least Favorite Secondary Color

3. They love to be nurtured by others.   T   F
4. They need to be more selfish.   T   F

Purple Favorite Secondary Color

5. They don't like talking about ideas or developing new things.   T   F
6. When insulted, they get quiet.   T   F

Purple Least Favorite Secondary Color

7. They show their emotions to everyone.   T   F
8. When upset, they say nothing.   T   F

Orange Favorite Secondary Color

9. When bored, they will create chaos.   T   F
10. They can be sentimental, even sappy.   T   F

Orange Least Favorite Secondary Color

11. They can be too nice.   T   F
12. They are good at eliminating what's not working.   T   F

*Answers on the next page

Answers to the Secondary IQ Quiz

Green Favorite Secondary Color

1. F   Don't let those sweet faces fool you.
2. T   They are having an intimate moment with your mind.

Green Least Favorite Secondary Color

3. T   Cooking them a meal is a big deal.
4. T   They could take selfish lessons.

Purple Favorite Secondary Color

5. F   They will give you their opinions even if you don't ask for them.
6. T   Then, they get even.

Purple Least Favorite Secondary Color

7. F   Even their lovers don't know them.
8. T   In a personal crisis, saying "Good morning" is an effort for them.

Orange Favorite Secondary Color

9. T   Watch out. Somehow they will get you to stir up the day.
10. T   Pictures and stories can be nonstop.

Orange Least Favorite Secondary Color

11. T   Listen to them: "Can I help you?"
12. F   They continue doing things the wrong way until they pass out.

CHAPTER FIFTEEN

Achromatics

Your Hopes and Fears

The significance of a man is not in what he attains but rather in what he longs to attain.
—KAHLIL GIBRAN

Black, brown, and white fall into the achromatic category because they are not in the visible colored rays of the chromatic spectrum. They represent your inner self. This instinctual part of you is the glue that holds you together. It is the underlying force behind all your hopes and fears. Before you begin, review your achromatic color selections from page 13.

In this chapter you'll learn how to allow the silence within you to exist. Working too hard, thinking too much, or substance abuse will make it difficult for you to experience your inner feelings.

Your favorite achromatic color represents your core, which rationally directs change. You are trying to make sure your inner self is getting what it needs most.

Your least favorite achromatic color symbolizes the deep-rooted concerns that inhibit the pursuit of your passions and signifies your particular way of making sure that your inner self is confronting your greatest dilemmas.

The achromatic colors indicate what your reaction will be when pressure is forcing you to change. You will see what you treasure most about yourself, as well as your greatest flaw. As you read this chapter, be especially tuned in to the voice inside of you that is only apparent when you are completely silent.

BLACK FAVORITE

> We function on feeling. When you know the magic, you will always find a place in the Kingdom.
> —WALT DISNEY

- **Key words:** emotional, focused, loyal
- **Power:** to know your emotions
- **Motivation:** to understand your past

Your Hopes

You know the value each person brings to a relationship. Others see you as an impetuous, forceful, self-protective person. You want to know about the unknown. You try to map your life into a logical plan for the future. At decision time, your feelings can override rationality.

Your commitment to others provides you with a healthy perspective of yourself. You passionately extend yourself to others. When you get too close and they reject you, your feelings play back an emotional review of your life. Contemplating past emotional feelings makes you feel secure and gives you the sense that you are on the right path.

Your Fears

You take people and events too seriously. This makes it hard, sometimes impossible, for you to remain objective. You tend to shift the blame onto someone or something else if things don't go your way. Much of your misery is caused by not letting go of the past. Retreating into your memories only compounds your problems.

When you become upset, you exaggerate your responsibilities and feel overwhelmed. Only when you're emotionally frustrated do you consider making changes. Starting a new course of action makes you feel guilty, as if you're betraying others or losing yourself.

Feed Your Soul

You find it sexy when others need you. It allows you to feel close to them, even safe. Being close to others makes you feel that the world cannot hurt you. When others encourage you to express how you feel, it turns you on.

You feel very responsible for those around you. This makes those you care about feel comfortable. They know where you stand. It can also, however, make you too predictable. If you don't already, make it a point to blow it out occasionally. Keep it spicy!

Unstuff Your Relationships

When you feel that others aren't giving you emotional support, you try to get even closer. Take a step back, and give them the space they need. Don't let your need to be emotionally attached push them away. If you feel pain, it is your denial to accept something that is surfacing. Don't be so needy. Your defensiveness will negatively affect your self-confidence and make it difficult for people to be close to you.

Getting It Done

You're disciplined and keep others in line. When you are loyal or have ownership, you fight to keep what is yours. You're an overachiever and need autonomy to be at your best. You like to get things finished without being interrupted. Still, you need for coworkers to be loyal to you, and, in turn, you are genuinely concerned about them.

Get Your Act Together

Your need to complete everything can hamper your ability to be open to essential information. This stubborn streak will be your downfall. Don't let your determination make you miss the obvious. Listen for new options, even after your decision is made. Let others contribute. Many times, new ways of doing things will actually complement your method.

Your Great Lesson

Your memories are the treasures of your spirit. They belong only to you. Honor them by not getting tangled up in your emotions. Learn from them and move forward.

BLACK LEAST FAVORITE: YOU MAKE
UNEMOTIONAL DECISIONS

You are very rational. At decision time, you are unemotional. This detachment helps you connect with new ideas and information. Using only logic, you can see where others are excessive and inconsistent. You cut to the truth to focus on what needs to be done.

In your relationships, you become very attached and your emotions overwhelm you. Completely losing yourself can be a major turn-on. Later, however, you can experience an empty feeling, as if you have lost yourself. Ending a relationship at first appears to be easy for you, but releasing the residual emotions from it is difficult. You need to understand that still having feelings after the fact doesn't mean you should go back and change your decision.

In the workplace, you are driven and desire advancement. You expect others to recognize your levelheaded way of doing business. You wish to make your own schedule without having to report to a superior. Under pressure, you become very logical-minded. This is the exact opposite of what happens in your relationships. When the pressure is really tough, coworkers seek you out for an unbiased perspective. Helping them solve their problems makes you feel special.

Get in touch with your emotions. Try not to be a rationalist all the time. If you follow your heart instead of your head, you will be happier in the long run. You'll better understand the value of your commitments, and any changes occurring in your life will fit your needs more readily. You will gain the power to better direct those "illogical feelings."

WHITE FAVORITE

> The only man who can change his mind is the man who's got one.
> —EDWARD NOYES WESTCOTT

- **Key words:** objective, curious, analytical
- **Power:** to see new options
- **Motivation:** to create a new future

Your Hopes

You give the gift of knowledge. Your suggestions make others slow down and consider all the options. Your objectivity gives you and others the ability to consider things thoroughly. When you get what you wish, your hope is renewed. You bring optimistic agendas and problem-solving skills to situations.

Your satisfaction is linked to navigating options successfully. You desire to better evaluate all things so that you can integrate them with your goals. The world is yours for the taking if you can distinguish subtle differences between choices. By logically analyzing things before taking action, you have the power to plot the future you want.

Your Fears

Under pressure, you step back to gain objectivity. However, too much distance can cause you to lose sight of what's important to you. It can keep you from making the best of existing situations. Slow down. Remember to give your feelings equal power. You will better know what you want. Your world will feel more solid.

Feed Your Soul

When you have enough space, everyone benefits. Having breathing room in your work environment and relationships gives you the power not to get bogged down with problems. You also gain the ability to tell people about new ways to make their lives better.

Unstuff Your Relationships

You have a tendency to avoid getting close to people. You immerse yourself in new schemes and overload yourself with information. Is it any wonder, then, that people can feel you are self-absorbed and not committed to them? Under stress they may even feel that you've severed your relationship with them without saying good-bye. Decide what makes you happy, and cleanly cut things from your life that aren't working. Allow your future to be determined by the actions you take, not by the results of your inaction.

Getting It Done

You are at your best when you can give advice on new and better ways of doing things. You adapt well to changing situations. Environments where you can meet new people and experience new things invigorate your natural curiosity. All this stimulation enhances your charm. It allows you to appreciate who and what is important to you.

Get Your Act Together

Don't let your search to find the perfect solution destroy your ability to make decisions. Be decisive. There are no guarantees in life. Failing to make timely decisions will only make matters worse. Constantly looking for new options can also make others feel as though they are unimportant in your estimation. They can lose their loyalty to you or feel that you do not have confidence in them. Make sure you make what is already working a priority.

Your Great Lesson

Clearly communicate your need for extra space in your relationships in order to see things objectively. Once others understand your nature, they will better appreciate your valuable suggestions.

WHITE LEAST FAVORITE:
YOU MAKE OTHERS FEEL THEY BELONG

When your spirit soars, you attract others like a magnet. Talking to you makes them feel that they belong. This helps you fit in. When you feel bad, change is almost impossible. Many times you retreat right before you try to end something. Your fear of abandonment can stop you from starting over, even when situations are harmful to you.

When you start to make a change in your life, you panic. You see too many options, which can make you feel confused or frustrated. This state is only temporary. Concentrate on distancing yourself from your fear. Don't worry; you won't lose what's important to you. In fact, you'll see more clearly what you value in life.

In comfortable work situations, your very presence makes things come together. Your energy inspires closer teamwork among coworkers. You run into trouble, however, when you do not consider all the options. Have you investigated and considered all your possible resources? Have you gotten input from the vendors, the department heads, and your coworkers? Be careful. If you wait until the last minute, you might miss opportunities or make extra work for yourself.

When you don't have to be thinking about someone or something else, you will know the pleasure of being alive. You will be able to take risks, see new things, and meet exciting people. Try imagining yourself lying on a beach. Who do you want there with you? Why? Who did not get invited? Why not? Knowing where you stand will allow you to feel a lot more secure.

BROWN FAVORITE

> The world is a looking glass and gives back to every
> man the reflection of his own face.
> —WILLIAM MAKEPEACE THACKERAY

- ■ *Key words:* aware, authentic, compassionate
- ■ *Power:* to understand reality
- ■ *Motivation:* to experience the sensations of life

Your Hopes

You are down-to-earth. By recognizing your superficial aspects, you become authentic. For the most part you do not believe in an afterlife, divine judgment, or cruel fate. Things just exist. Everything else is vanity. You are able to weigh all the available options, thinking twice before making a decision. Others might see you as intuitive. But in reality you are simply free of illusions and well aware of the consequences of your actions.

You prefer to live in the moment and appreciate the pleasures of life. You are inspired by the charms of the world. The more you experience your environment, the more you express yourself. Doing is exciting. Activity makes you feel more complete. You are constantly looking for new sensations to spice up your life.

Your Fears

Your fears are based on physical realities. Death, decay, aging, and loss of faculties and happiness are your concerns. You worry that your dedication has caused you to neglect important areas of your own life. Then, when you declare what you want, others can see you as selfish. Step back before you act. Notice how each person contributes to your life. Does he or she respect your knowledge? Is your loyalty appreciated?

Feed Your Soul

You wish to indulge your passions and live to the fullest. You often have an exaggerated look of concentration in

your eyes. Your strong awareness of others' needs creates
energy. It turns you on and allows you to get what or whom
you want. This is your power. You don't take things personally and refrain from judgment. You realize that each person
is out for him- or herself. That's just the way of life.

Unstuff Your Relationships

When upset, you can become fixated on what you want,
determined to get it no matter what the consequences are. Is
your dedication to people or projects keeping you from
experiencing your own desires? Before you grab for what
you want, confront your feelings. Otherwise, your obsessive
nature can cause people to feel neglected and to question
their worth to you.

Getting It Done

As a manager, you fully comprehend situations before issuing commands. You prefer to work in an environment
where you can be very supportive and keep others aware of
the day-to-day realities. Your realistic thinking helps you
make the most out of physical resources. You think about
making things better now, not later, and don't dwell on the
past. Others are comforted by your keen awareness.

Get Your Act Together

When you constantly ask questions to try to ascertain the
facts, others can assume you are less knowledgeable than
you really are. They don't understand you're trying to cut
through everyone's subjective viewpoint. This is a big con-

cern and could lead to your being passed over and denied the recognition you deserve. Make sure to let others know what you've accomplished.

Your Great Lesson

Don't try to be everything to those you are committed to. Instead, focus on being deeply involved and committed to experiencing your life. You'll become more alive.

BROWN LEAST FAVORITE: NOTHING CAN STOP YOU

You're an alumnus of the school of hard knocks. By learning the hard way, you have experienced things you never would have if things had been easier. You are determined to make changes. You feel that you can change your environment and yourself and nothing can stop you.

As you get older, you notice things are different. Everyone has gotten older. Don't obsess about time creeping up on you. Accept that your viewpoint will change, you will look older, and some younger people will not find you as sexy. Enjoy yourself at each stage of your life.

You can sometimes feel that you are aggressively pushing yourself to get what you want and are going nowhere, or that you've spent too long waging everyone else's battles. Look again. Aren't you avoiding facts that you know all too well? At first, becoming more aware of what you're capable of and what you can expect from your relationships will feel like an ice-cold shower. Later, however, you will feel marvelous, more alive.

At work, you can ask too much of yourself or others. Take things as they come. Do not expect others to protect you. You'll feel more grounded and more in control. Be honest with yourself and accept limitations. Denying what capabilities a job or career requires will only frustrate you in the end. You won't be any wiser from the experience.

Ultimately, life is only as rich as your experiences. Regularly remind yourself that you are going to die. You will treasure more what you are doing and attract friends and relationships that will allow you to savor life more deeply.

PREDICTING OUTCOMES

The combination of your favorite and least favorite achromatic color selections shows how you confront change.

Black Favorite, White Least Favorite

You rely on your emotional awareness to improve your relationships. You are very dedicated, and your loyalty to those around you makes you greatly loved. Unfortunately, when a change is needed, you have a tendency to dwell on things excessively. You can get stuck in one mind-set or obsess about a relationship long after it has ended. Prioritize what is important, and then go out and make your own luck.

Black Favorite, Brown Least Favorite

Your emotions make you feel powerful. Regardless of the distractions in life, you see the value of things. Your loyalty to others helps them become better people, which is probably why you have such devoted people around you. However, when making decisions, you sometimes have unrealistic expectations of others. So be careful. Accept things as they are, not how they could be, and people will not let you down as much. Your life will be more satisfying. You will feel more like a winner.

White Favorite, Black Least Favorite

Logical and practical, you easily find new ways of achieving your goals. But because you keep your emotions tightly under wrap and maintain your distance, people can find you cold. Being of a critical nature doesn't help you either. At first, you may find it hard to get close to someone in a relationship. You feel as if you are losing your objectivity. Later, however, you become completely dedicated, able to offer nonstop clever suggestions.

White Favorite, Brown Least Favorite

You constantly assess yourself and others. However, the options that you see for yourself are often beyond your ability to accomplish or may not be what you really want. You spend too much energy on the search and not enough thought about where you really want to go. Distancing yourself from your feelings and other people doesn't help any. Are you afraid to confront your desires? Deal with them. Determine where they will lead you, or you will destroy your ability to hold on to what is most important to you.

Brown Favorite, Black Least Favorite

You are very realistic. It is difficult to fool you. You base your decisions on the facts. At the start others see you as concerned about them. But all of a sudden, you seem only to care about what's right and not about people's feelings. You are an overachiever, but all this activity can get in the way of understanding yourself. Remember that you are more than just the sum of your achievements. Confront your emotions. Otherwise, you will only define yourself in respect to how others see you.

Brown Favorite, White Least Favorite

You are very realistic and have an innate sense of fairness. You use facts to pull things together. Others think of you as being very sensitive to their issues and needs. Regrettably, all of this attention paid to others distracts you from thinking about yourself. Be more objective. Take a moment to decide what else you could have in life, or your obsessive routines will destroy your future.

SEXUAL CHEMISTRY

If your partner selected . . .

The same favorite achromatic color as you did, he or she enables you to better piece together your inner self and makes you feel good about yourself.

A different favorite achromatic color than you did, he or she makes you aware of your greatest lessons in life and gives you the knowledge to succeed.

A Black with a Black

Both partners have a genuine appreciation of how loyal each is to those the other cares about. Together you make each other feel good about the decisions and sacrifices you've made in your lives on behalf of other people or for the sake of your relationship. You need each other.

When upset, though, neither of you listens to the other. Together you can become paranoid, both expecting the worst. Constantly dwelling on situations or on other people is really a waste of your energy.

A White with a White

You two mutually supply the freedom each needs to do what you want in life. Together you harness your objective, curious, analytical abilities to solve problems. Both of you admire the other's ability to be independent. This autonomy empowers each of you to stay focused on your future without interference.

When there is a crisis, you both need space. A conflict creates a time lapse in which your fast thinking can be a waste of both of your energies.

A Brown with a Brown

This duo creates a world all their own when they first meet. Together, your compassionate awareness creates an authentic environment where you both can appreciate the pleasures of life. You talk about how to make your work fun or your home more comfortable. Others see you as free of illusions and aware of the consequences of your actions.

Doing is exciting for you both. However, one of you can become overly dedicated to someone or something else or become fixated on something you want. Your compulsive determination to reach your goal can make the other partner feel neglected.

A Black with a White

You make good decisions together. As a black, you talk about your feelings. This openness makes a white feel more comfortable with emotions and generally more secure. As a white, you objectively calm your emotional partner, enabling the black to see new options and to look before leaping.

In a crisis, as a white, you "back off" to objectively view the situation. The black in turn pushes forward, attempting to get even closer to you. You then feel closed in and tend to view the black as being too needy. Consequently, you retreat even more. The result is a clash, good conversation, or great sex.

A Black with a Brown

This couple creates action-oriented passion. As a black, you challenge a brown to contemplate what's most important. Your concerns encourage the brown to accumulate more wealth or see more value in your relationship. In a crisis, the black's emotions can discount practical solutions—a major frustration to the brown.

As a brown, you keep the black from hitting brick

walls. Your intuitiveness teaches your partner to come back down to earth and concentrate on current practicalities, not past emotions. You can become consumed, however, by what you're doing. This can make the black feel like an afterthought in your life.

A White with a Brown

You discover new possibilities to enjoy with each other. As a white, you help a brown move forward in relationships and career by offering a steady flow of suggestions. You appreciate how the brown grounds you in both your relationship and the world outside it. In a personal crisis, however, you can view your partner as engaging in limited thinking, which makes the brown feel unneeded.

As a brown, your dedication and sharp awareness are a constant source of stimulation for the white. Your observations create an ongoing stream of useful information. You make each day fun—full of action. When you don't feel appreciated, you start helping others who need you. This shift can leave the white feeling unnoticed and discarded.

YOUR ACHROMATIC BOUNDARIES

Your need for personal space creates emotional boundaries. When someone stands back too far, you feel that he or she has abandoned you. If someone gets too close, you can feel that he or she is imposing on you. This continual back-and-forth game of creating distance one moment and being uncomfortably close the next is a lifelong struggle to be intimate with someone yet not lose yourself.

Choose your favorite achromatic color between only black and white. You will learn how you are handling your personal space.

If you prefer black, you push forward. Your emotions make others feel your presence. This can irritate or stimulate your partner. You create an intense feeling of closeness by eliminating emotional distance. Being closer makes your relationship more intimate for you.

If you prefer white, you step back to preserve your space and maintain your objectivity. This motivates the intimacy-seeking blacks to move closer. This seesaw movement creates exciting energy. It stimulates new thoughts and feelings.

When you both like black or white, things get a bit crazy. If both of you like black, one is forced outside of his or her comfort zone. One of you must become distant and more objective, like a white. The reverse is also true. If you both like white, one is forced outside of his or her comfort zone to become closer, more intimate like a black.

Laughing Out Loud

Awareness of nonverbal communication is not only essential— it's fun! Play a spatial-boundary game with your friends or partner to see what I mean. The only rule is to do the opposite of what you normally do. Then, watch as the other person becomes uncomfortable.

If you prefer black, create spatial distance by standing away and being more objective. Watch your friend become warmer or your partner become more lovey-dovey.

If you prefer white, stand closer than normal and be

more emotional. Watch your friend or partner become more objective, less emotional.

Your friend or partner will unconsciously assume your normal role, and chances are he or she won't like it at all. Afterward, tell him or her what you have done. Understanding this powerful, nonverbal communication will strengthen your relationships and get a lot of laughs. You will become aware of the glue that bonds you and your loved ones together.

THE LANGUAGE OF ACHROMATIC COLORS

Black Is Feeling Emotion

Black is the absence of light. Close your eyes, and your awareness will go inward to feel your past. In the darkness, your thoughts consider what or who has been important to you. You gain the power to know your feelings and gauge the value of each person or situation.

White Is Seeing Options

White is light itself. Light gives you knowledge of the world around you. It gives you the freedom to rise beyond yourself or a predicament to learn new information. You gain the power to objectively view new options for your future.

Brown Is Realizing Authenticity

Brown is the earthy existence of the flesh. In accepting, not fabricating, the bold realities of each person or situation, you see their authenticity. You gain the power to see the far-reaching implications of each action or decision.

When Your Achromatic Colors Change

Should you find yourself drawn to a new achromatic color, you are questioning the very core of your existence. When your favorite achromatic color changes, you will feel indecisive, as if you are on shaky ground. A change in your least favorite achromatic color shows you are reevaluating your entire perspective on life. These changes are temporary. They give you the ability to gather more information, but make the tough decisions more difficult.

The Achromatic IQ Quiz

Answer True or False.

Black Favorite Achromatic Color

1. They hang on in a relationship till they drop.   T   F
2. They're never emotional.   T   F

Black Least Favorite Achromatic Color

3. They're not the people to whom you should exaggerate.   T   F
4. At decision time they're concerned with how you feel.   T   F

Brown Favorite Achromatic Color

5. They can sometimes be seen as insincere.   T   F
6. They can become stubborn if they want something.   T   F

Brown Least Favorite Achromatic Color

7. They love to tell you how old they are.   T   F
8. They can be virgins and tell you how
   to have great sex.   T   F

White Favorite Achromatic Color

9. They coined the phrase "I need space."   T   F
10. They see freedom as no big thing.   T   F

White Least Favorite Achromatic Color

11. They panic when there is emotional
    change.   T   F
12. They don't care if they fit in.   T   F

*Answers on the next page

Answers to the Achromatic IQ Quiz

Black Favorite Achromatic Color

1. T Saying good-bye is a dramatic event for them.
2. F Feelings direct their lives.

Black Least Favorite Achromatic Color

3. T Your drama will be a joke to them.
4. F Once the decision is final, they're cold.

Brown Favorite Achromatic Color

5. F They're the real McCoys.
6. T They never outgrew the terrible twos.

Brown Least Favorite Achromatic Color

7. F If they're over thirty, don't even ask.
8. T They don't acknowledge that you need to experience it before you understand it.

White Favorite Achromatic Color

9. T "Close" to them isn't that close.
10. F It's everything to them.

White Least Favorite Achromatic Color

11. T They freeze. Only later will they talk about it.
12. F They make everything fit—even if it doesn't.

CHAPTER SIXTEEN

Intermediates

Taking On the World

I believe the future is only the past again, entered through another gate.
—ARTHUR WING PINERO

Lime green, teal, indigo, magenta, red-orange, and gold are in the intermediate-color category. They represent how you approach the world. These energized hues spark you to act or react. They give you the different perspectives you need to direct your life. Get ready to view the ups and downs of your day! Review your intermediate color selections from page 13.

In this chapter, you'll learn what your two favorite intermediate colors indicate about your approach to getting something you want. In an up moment, your selections reveal how you achieve success. You will read how your confident self engages the world. Contemplate this aspect of yourself, and success will be yours.

Your two least favorite intermediate colors show the perspectives you tend to forget. In a down moment, they disclose what you need to do yet have never considered.

The intermediate colors show how you make requests. Lime green, indigo, and red-orange push forward to inform you of what is needed. Magenta, teal, and gold lean back to create a space for you to see what is required. Both styles can be equally aggressive. As you read this chapter, look around you. Have fun watching others act out these visible characteristics.

LIME GREEN FAVORITE

> It takes a very unusual mind to undertake the
> analysis of the obvious.
> —ALFRED NORTH WHITEHEAD

- *Key words:* logical, self-investigative
- *Initiates:* rational ways of doing things
- *Concern:* What else do I need?

In the Beginning

You are incessantly contemplating what is missing in your life. You think about how it would feel to have certain things. Your strong sense of logic and no-nonsense style help people get to the heart of a matter. Even if they don't ask for help, eventually you will tell others what they need to do. Sometimes it seems so obvious, you can't help but blurt it out. You'll say exactly what other people are most afraid to hear. You recognize the consequences of avoiding essential needs.

You in Action

Use your logic to pinpoint the questions that need to be asked. Knowing the pertinent questions is as important as knowing the answers. Be the inventive person that you were meant to be. Don't let a misstep stop you from being a winner. Guide yourself, your projects, and those on your team to new methods or better ways of doing things.

Your Highs

Your steady consideration of what you want allows you to exert logical control over what you start. You're seeking more change and adventure in life. Once you begin something, you don't quit. You grasp all the details needed for you to achieve your vision. This talent gives you an advantage in conversations and relationships. Others see you as a fast-thinking self-starter.

Your Lows

You can become extremely introverted and get lost in your thoughts. When others fail to see what you've come to understand, you feel that you don't fit in. Sometimes you become consumed with your thoughts about what other people really need. Don't be so full of yourself. Answers are not always available and others' needs are not going to be the same as yours. Go back and examine the period before your intense involvement in a project or relationship began. Why did you start it in the first place? Then, clearly communicate your thoughts about what you need to discover. Others will understand more readily what's needed to perform well on your team.

The Seductive You

At first, you are a tough cookie, a hard person to get close to. Once you have accepted an individual, however, you get emotional about him or her and all your logic disappears. You become dedicated. When you are just starting a relationship, your forthright nature can be seen as sexy. Everyone notices you when you walk into the room.

Your Healing Force

Your inward focus motivates others to contemplate what they really need.

LIME GREEN LEAST FAVORITE: YOU HAVE BAD TIMING

You tend to avoid looking inside yourself to view what is missing in your life. Your refusal to be introspective can lead to frustration. You deny your needs for so long that eventually you just explode.

The good news is that you can find yourself in the middle of all kinds of adventures. The bad news is that the adventures don't meet your needs; they're simply what was available to you.

Initially you can avoid meeting "Mr. or Ms. Right," or confronting what you need from your present mate. Then all of a sudden, you quickly meet someone or become overwhelmed about what is missing in your current relationship. This erratic behavior makes it difficult for you to know if what you have is what you want. It can send out confusing signals to your suitor or partner.

When you find yourself repeatedly avoiding something you want, regard the behavior as a warning sign. You need to take the time to ponder your repressed thoughts. Only then will you recognize the rewards and consequences of accepting something or letting someone new into your life. Bad timing can waste a lot of your energy.

MAGENTA FAVORITE

> Still round the corner there may wait / A new road or secret gate . . .
> —J. R. R. TOLKIEN

- **Key words:** enthusiastic, socially investigative
- **Initiates:** attracting new people and situations
- **Concern:** Where or with whom can I become inspired?

In the Beginning

You surround yourself with friends who challenge you to grow. Your mind is seldom at rest. You are searching for inspiration and a sense of magic in your relationships and undertakings. The world is your oyster, and you know how to get the most out of it for yourself and others. You have a genuine desire to bring about positive change.

You in Action

Use your enthusiasm to regenerate yourself and those around you. Getting excited about what you already enjoy releases unlimited passion. Opportunities will seem just to appear. Teach your coworkers and loved ones to window-shop—to concentrate on looking and not buying in to any one person or situation. They will see new avenues that will create more results with less effort.

Your Highs

You regenerate people. You have the power to spark new possibilities. Your need to believe in people helps them to believe in themselves. What they have longed to do becomes something they can do. You help others to see what will work for them.

Your Lows

When you don't prioritize, you initiate new things without finishing what you have already started. Many of your ideas might have been brilliant, if only they'd been realized. Herein lies your frustration. To cope with it, you need to seek help to complete your tasks. After all, you didn't really want to finish all those projects you started, anyway. Contemplate your feelings. Realize that you don't need to take on new projects to keep from becoming bored. Completing things can be very exciting and rewarding. If you're able to say no to starting something new, that's half the battle.

The Seductive You

Sometimes you are surprised at all the people you attract in life. You're an enchanter. Your body language entices others and then you're off together on an adventure.

You can't help but start something new in your relationships. You bring a certain sense of openness and curiosity to social situations. Your enthusiasm makes each day an event.

Your Healing Force

Your curiosity galvanizes others to open their minds and see the opportunities in the world around them.

MAGENTA LEAST FAVORITE: YOU ARE SUSPICIOUS

You need to feel inspired, but it is difficult for you. You're suspicious of new things. When you meet someone, your questioning nature can make others feel uncomfortable. Don't second-guess life. Be open to the idea that others are who they appear to be until proven otherwise.

You attract others who are inspired by their environment. Their enthusiasm opens up your life. They force you to reveal your dreams to yourself. Recognize that you are going to start new things, or you will lose control.

When your energy is down, however, pay attention to your body language. If you are not looking forward to doing something or being with someone, it would be best for everyone, including you, to stay home.

Relax. Risk experiencing new things. Surround yourself with people who inspire you. Smile more and you'll find yourself having a lot more fun. New adventures will suddenly present themselves.

TEAL FAVORITE

> Tact is the intelligence of the heart.
> —ANONYMOUS

- *Key words:* social worth, empathy
- *Initiates:* respect for accomplishments
- *Concern:* Do others think well of me?

In the Beginning

You seek to develop your self-esteem. Use your excellent communication skills and ability to empathize with other people's points of view. A great diplomat, you build people up by actively listening and giving them positive feedback. You want to help others become everything they want to be. This behavior makes you feel important, as well, and helps you fit in.

You in Action

Determine what specific skills are required to complete a task so that you will see how to accomplish it. Many times, believing in your own capability is mostly about knowing exactly what to do. Simply focus on listening for the positive rhythm inside yourself and others. Your strong belief, like magic, makes your own and others' wishes come true.

Your Highs

Sometimes you get up in the morning and feel like the most important person in the world. You feel you have the capabilities to accomplish whatever you want. You see your dreams within your grasp. Your past achievements become personal victories that make you proud.

Your Lows

Other times you feel as if you are not important at all, that you are pleasing others, not yourself. This can make it difficult for you to be creative. Stop being so concerned with what others think. Be honest with yourself. Muster the courage to speak up even when others do not want to listen. You will gain trust and respect from your peers. They will see you as more authentic.

The Seductive You

You are very endearing. Sensitivity to other people's needs helps you to start new relationships. You try to become what the other person is looking for. You boost his or her confidence. This makes you very attractive.

Yet your concerns about what others think can keep you from being completely honest. In your desire to be accepted, you sometimes say what people want to hear instead of how you feel. Later on, they're in for a shock when your actions don't reflect your words. Being forthcoming about your own needs will go a long way toward making others feel comfortable with you.

Your Healing Force

Your belief in others' dreams makes them believe in themselves.

TEAL LEAST FAVORITE: YOU ARE SKEPTICAL

You work very, very hard because you have a deep need to show you are competent. You may tell yourself that you don't care about what others think, but this is just a defensive ploy.

When you voice or feel skepticism, that's when you get into trouble and you later regret what you said or the impression you have conveyed. Even though you might have been right, was there anything gained by being negative?

People know where they stand with you. Many times this makes those close to you feel comfortable in their relationship with you. Others might hear, sometimes for the first time, how you perceive them. Your outspoken, skeptical nature can also make it difficult to get close to you. Give people the opportunity to say what they really believe to be true before you even think about offering your own opinion.

Encourage others to seek their dream even when you don't believe in it. Remember, their dreams are about them, not you. Appreciate their positive energy. You'll become more optimistic about your own wishes.

RED-ORANGE FAVORITE

> There is a road from the eye to the heart that does not
> go through the intellect.
> —G. K. CHESTERTON

- ■ *Key words:* personal worth, self-respect
- ■ *Initiates:* respect for the individual
- ■ *Concern:* Am I respected?

In the Beginning

You value the individual's right to a sense of dignity. By immersing yourself in life, you are able to see what clicks and what does not. Your ability to commit yourself to a person makes him or her trust you. You appreciate the beauty of a person by making the time to be with him or her.

You in Action

Use your sharp eye to monitor what is actually occurring around you. Set limits and establish standards that ensure each person's honor and respect. Allow your unselfish devotion to make each individual feel worthwhile, and you will become stronger. Others will feel your strength and gain the willpower to celebrate people for what they do, not for what they say or even think. Go ahead. Make the world around you more authentic.

Your Highs

When you let your spirit flourish and show your sensitivity, your personal growth soars. You're able to appreciate what you have earned through your diligent efforts and make equitable comparisons of your current circumstances and relationships with those of your past. You make things work, even if all the ingredients for a solution aren't there.

By making aggressive suggestions about how to improve the lives of others, you exhibit your greatest attribute—true warmth in personal relationships. You appreciate each person for who he or she is.

Your Lows

In situations in which you feel a personal slight or injustice against you or someone else, you take things too personally. Even though your reaction is justified, don't become over-protective, critical, or even enraged. Compassion is more appropriate than anger. People have their own problems and baggage to handle.

The Seductive You

You are a loyal lover. This is very vital to your continued existence. When things aren't working, you know it. You forcefully try to ensure the trust and respect you deserve. You need an environment in which you can be respected for your true self. You are happiest when you have a few good friends and a partner who idolizes you.

You love one-on-one relationships and pets because you need to experience unconditional love. When you talk to the people you care about, you often touch them with your hands. Touch allows you to trust. Be cautious, though. Others can misunderstand your affection as sexual aggressiveness.

Your Healing Force

Your need to be respected encourages others to respect themselves.

RED-ORANGE LEAST FAVORITE: YOU FORGET YOURSELF

You immerse yourself in being there for those you care about. You may accomplish your goal, but in the end you are no closer to understanding what makes you happy. Do you sometimes wonder where you stop and others begin?

Touch is a very personal thing with you. In your behavioral response to it, you either openly embrace it or avoid it for the most part. However, you do have an emotional need to be touched, held, and appreciated for the beauty inside you.

Others can see your request for affection as sexual seductiveness or a need for attention. Express your vulnerability to those who care about you. You might be surprised to find a lot more love than criticism.

Be more authentic to yourself. Pay more attention to who you are, not to who you think you need to be. Feelings of being unloved will go away, and you will be able to express your true warmth. Otherwise, you'll lose out and feel like a victim.

INDIGO FAVORITE

> The world stands aside to let anyone pass who knows
> where they are going.
> —DAVID STARR JORDON

- ■ *Key words:* conceptual, self-confident
- ■ *Initiates:* beginnings of constructive ideas
- ■ *Concern:* Can I create a workable plan?

In the Beginning

You are focused on improving the future. Figuring out how to make your ideas a reality turns you on. Seeing things through to completion is the ultimate high. It gives you self-confidence.

When you're focused on developing an idea, you have the capacity to be the central, dramatic figure whom people gather around. This directness makes you a natural leader. When you're in top form, no one questions your authority.

You in Action

Use your futuristic thinking to create orchestrated plans. Put your doubts aside. Charge ahead with your inspirations. Discuss your idea with those around you. Revamp your original concept into a workable plan based on a consensus of exactly what is needed. Then jump right in, considering constantly if there is a better way to realize your aim or even if you need assistance from someone else. Your unwavering focus will radiate self-confidence and propel you to success.

Your Highs

Sometimes you have so much self-confidence, you feel you can save the world. You love initiating new ideas, and you safeguard their success by considering everything that can possibly go wrong. You assume that you can make things work. You are on a fast track to success. Others believe in you.

Your Lows

When your energy is down, even making toast becomes an act of courage. You have no self-confidence and feel scattered. During these low periods, you need a lot of attention. When people believe in you, you begin to believe in yourself. Many times friends help you to realize that your feelings of disappointment are from having unrealistic expectations.

The Seductive You

Your commanding, dramatic approach to things makes you appear very romantic. At times, however, you can be in love with the idea of love. This can make you see people the way you want them to be, not the way they are. Initially, your dream person will meet all your expectations, but once you are romantically involved, you will see him or her as he or she really is, warts and all.

You have a tendency to be self-involved. This makes

those who care about you feel insignificant in your eyes. Connect with others and keep your expectations realistic.

Your Healing Force

Your deep need to plan your life inspires others to invest more in themselves.

INDIGO LEAST FAVORITE: YOU PROCRASTINATE

Your fly-by-the-seat-of-your-pants mode is thrilling, but can get you in loads of trouble. Not making plans can create turmoil, and later you feel somewhat lost—without direction. Others might misinterpret your wishy-washy behavior, making matters even worse.

Don't procrastinate. Go ahead, plan your future. But first, you'll need a deeper level of commitment. If you just go through the motions and try to keep up appearances, you will never achieve your goals. You will not be able to combine your resources and talents effectively and miss out on fun things.

At first you will have a powerful, emotional connection with your "dream person." You see only the things you like and avoid looking at who he or she really is. You become completely immersed in the other person's plan. This can place you in a lot of situations that only appear fun. Avoid romantic disappointments by not being so quick to act.

Recognize that it's easier to start new things when you can visualize what you want. Conduct an investigation. Piece together a plan for your future. Say exactly what you're going to do. You will become more focused on success and worry less about failure.

GOLD FAVORITE

> In playing, we discover the essence of who we are.
> —ANONYMOUS

- ■ *Key words:* resourceful, playful
- ■ *Initiates:* release of undesirable thoughts
- ■ *Concern:* What am I enjoying?

In the Beginning

Life is a game to be played. You demand a stimulating environment and the time to enjoy it. Meeting new people, discovering what your friends are thinking, and studying your surroundings are ways you gather information. With a probing curiosity, you uncover what you want and how to get it. Ideas come together to create new possibilities.

You in Action

Use your foresight to see the value in each and every resource. Playfully examine each thing around you. Let your mind be free to associate the usability of resources or talents. Make sure that you pause to communicate how you made or connected things together into workable situations. Your fast-thinking mind and uncanny ability to use resources can easily be overlooked. Document how you created exciting new things from nothing, and expect admiration.

Your Highs

Downtime gives you the power to eliminate distractions and rediscover what you enjoy. Methodically, you gather information. You see truths impartially and encourage others to talk about what they enjoy. Experiencing their passions mentally stimulates you. You can make people get really excited about doing something they generally would not do.

Your Lows

Overemphasis on fun distracts you from achieving more meaningful relationships. Making too many plans can be a way of avoiding emotional issues. You're so busy looking for the next thrill that you often forget to appreciate what you already have.

The Seductive You

You see dating and courtship as an adventure. You experience different things and meet new people with an explosive spurt of energy. That's how you discover what's important to you in a relationship. But if you are not careful, your curiosity can get you into situations that you will later regret. Follow your natural inclination to get to know a person before getting too serious.

Your Healing Force

Your excitement about the fun you've planned stirs passion-ate desire in others to do something new.

GOLD LEAST FAVORITE:
YOU FORGET WHAT'S FUN

You keep very busy. You follow a rigorous schedule to avoid thinking about what is not working in your life. This rugged pace runs down your battery and makes it difficult for you to know what you really want to do. Others can even see you as rigid.

You attract others who are full of passion. In seeking to learn what you will enjoy, you listen to what others enjoy. Their interesting stories or the passion in their voices gets you excited. Their fun suggestions allow you to enjoy a day without your agendas. Be careful. Don't get caught up in their agendas. Do what's fun for you.

Avoid always asking serious questions. Instead, con-sider exaggerating your dilemma until you laugh. You will gain the objectivity to see beyond all the work you must do. Others will see you as less controlling and more fun.

Take a day off to relax and be free from responsibili-ties. Go play! Try not to watch television, read, or even answer the phone. At first, you will feel uncomfortable. Later, however, you will gain an inner awareness that will eliminate undesirable thoughts and incidentals from your life.

COLOR COMMENTARY

Are you mostly thoughtful or action-oriented? Rank the six intermediate colors below in order of most to least favorite (1 = most, 6 = least).

Row #1   Magenta _____   Teal _____   Gold _____
Row #2 Lime Green _____   Red-Orange _____   Indigo _____

Now, consider only your top three favorites. How many are in Row #1? Row #2?

Row #1 _____ (Magenta, Teal, Gold)
Row #2 _____ (Lime Green, Red-Orange, Indigo)

If you selected two of your top three favorites from . . .

Row #1, you are mostly thoughtful.
Row #2, you are mostly action-oriented.

Read the following descriptions of what constitutes a thoughtful or an action-oriented personality.

THOUGHTFUL

You are primarily concerned with your thoughts. You consider how another person or a situation affects you, and your considerations draw people in. Simply stated, when you think about someone, he or she thinks about you. You are inspiring. This is especially true if you selected all of your top three favorite intermediates from Row #1.

Sometimes it is best for you to "just do it." You will never know what you want until you try reaching for it.

ACTION-ORIENTED

You prefer taking action rather than waiting for things to come. Your focus on doing what you want attracts those who need change. Your constant motion forces others to move, too. You motivate others to do for themselves. This is especially true if you selected all of your top three favorites from Row #2.

Sometimes it is best for you to let life come to you. Be more thoughtful about what you want before you act, and your life will be richer.

Laughing Out Loud

Extremes attract extremes. Wherever you are out of balance, you attract people and situations that give or teach you exactly what you need to know. These lessons can be inspiring, life-altering, even horrifying.

Consider how your thoughts and actions have attracted the most wonderful and also the most terrifying person or situation.

When Your Intermediate Colors Change

Your intermediate colors change more than any of the other colors. When your goals change, your color choices often change, too. Get really mad or really happy, and you'll see an immediate change in your intermediate-color preferences. For the most part, however, your favorite and least favorite colors remain constant.

THE LANGUAGE OF INTERMEDIATE COLOR

How each intermediate color articulates into language is described below.

Lime Green Is Self-Investigation

Yellow (the search for a realistic perspective) and green (nurturing) combine to make lime green. Together they generate the power to question what is missing in your life.

Teal Is Believing in Your Future

Green (nurturing) and blue (future-based planning) combine to make teal. Together they generate the power to nurture and believe in your dreams.

Indigo Is Creating a Plan

Blue (future-based planning) and purple (seeing possibilities) combine to make indigo. Together they generate the power to plan an exciting future.

Magenta Is Becoming Inspired

Purple (seeing possibilities) and red (directing resources) combine to make magenta. Together they generate the power to be inspired and help you enthusiastically embrace the world around you.

Red-Orange Is Self-Respect

Red (directing resources) and orange (dissecting out what is not working) combine to make red-orange. Together they generate the power to respect your individuality.

Gold Is Regeneration of Your Soul

Orange (dissecting out what is not working) and yellow (the search for a realistic perspective) combine to make gold. Together they generate the power to play and discover the essence of your passions.

The Intermediate IQ Quiz

Answer True or False.

Lime Green Favorite Intermediate Color

1. They ask a lot of questions.　　　　T　　F

Lime Green Least Favorite Intermediate Color

2. They always accept what they need.　　T　　F

Magenta Favorite Intermediate Color

3. They love finishing what they start.　　T　　F

Magenta Least Favorite Intermediate Color

4. They are difficult to inspire.　　　　T　　F

Red-Orange Favorite Intermediate Color

5. They can become concerned with high society.　　　　　　　　　　　　T　　F

Red-Orange Least Favorite Intermediate Color

6. They are seeking unconditional love.   T   F

Teal Favorite Intermediate Color

7. They are great listeners.   T   F

Teal Least Favorite Intermediate Color

8. They work harder and harder to recognize their accomplishments.   T   F

Indigo Favorite Intermediate Color

9. They appear very confident.   T   F

Indigo Least Favorite Intermediate Color

10. They aren't concerned about planning the future.   T   F

Gold Favorite Intermediate Color

11. They are all work and no play.   T   F

Gold Least Favorite Intermediate Color

12. They are very busy.   T   F

*Answers on the next page

Answers to the Intermediate IQ Quiz

Lime Green Favorite Intermediate Color

1.   T   They need to know all the facts.

Lime Green Least Favorite Intermediate Color

2.   F   No, no, no. Or is that yes, yes, yes?

Magenta Favorite Intermediate Color

3.   F   New is more fun.

Magenta Least Favorite Intermediate Color

4.   T   Their suspicious nature can border on paranoia.

Red-Orange Favorite Intermediate Color

5.   F   A few good friends are more important than an expensive bottle of champagne.

Red-Orange Least Favorite Intermediate Color

6.   T   They hide it really well.

Teal Favorite Intermediate Color

7.   T   Communication comes naturally to them.

Teal Least Favorite Intermediate Color

8.   T   Even being president of the United States is not enough.

Indigo Favorite Intermediate Color

9.   T   Much more than they really are.

Indigo Least Favorite Intermediate Color

10.   T   Least-favorite indigos are terrified of it.

Gold Favorite Intermediate Color

11.   F   When left alone, trouble is brewing.

Gold Least Favorite Intermediate Color

12.   T   Fun takes a lot of work.

Part Four

*Making Each Moment
a Celebration of You*

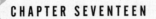

CHAPTER SEVENTEEN

Change Your Life, Not Yourself

*You cannot separate the good from
the bad and perhaps there is
no need to do so.*
—JACQUELINE KENNEDY ONASSIS

You need all the colors. Muster the courage to cherish and embrace all fifteen of them. Use them as your guide. You will gain strength—a more centered, stronger inner balance. Your new awareness will give you the muscle to make your life a passionate adventure.

You are nearing the end of your self-empowering journey. Consider, as you read, how the unspoken power of each color affects the complicated issues in your life.

In this chapter you will contemplate the colors you prefer in order to see your strengths. Look again, and you will see where you are stubborn, even arrogant.

You will also examine the colors you least prefer in order to celebrate what your past experiences have taught you. They will also indicate the areas of your life where you feel uncomfortable.

Truth Is Simple

Truth is always simple. If you think that you are complicated, chances are you are avoiding the fascinating inner workings that make up your personality. Stay focused on how you feel, not on what you think or do, or even what others say.

Don't let past experiences cloud your perspective. If you feel a relationship or some other situation is difficult to understand, you are not aware of, or accepting, all of the facts.

Empower Your Conversation

The goal of the Dewey Color System is to give you an awareness of how you prioritize the values and goals in your life. In learning the rewards and consequences of the way you set priorities, you gain the power to manage and direct your personality, focus on your passions, and realize your potential.

Create a real conversation. Talk with your children, spouse, parents, or team members at work about their favorite colors. Understanding how they prioritize the elements of their lives will enable you to be more patient about things that bother you and more appreciative of what they contribute to your learning.

THE COLOR COUNTDOWN

You are about to experience the color countdown, a condensed, in-depth summary of all fifteen colors. Your colors and life priorities are the same. Color was simply used as a way to access you, without the interference of language.

In reviewing the great power of each color in the

Dewey Color System, feel the passion and power within you. Use this spectrum-ordered summary to better link your thoughts and elevate your quality of life.

As you read the color countdown, be aware of the order in which you selected your colors. It determines your process of creating empowering change within yourself. You will gain insightful clues that will give you the awareness to better direct and manage your life.

THE FIFTEEN GREAT POWERS

Lime Green	Question it.
Green	Be it.
Teal	Believe it.
Blue	Dream it.
Indigo	Plan it.
Purple	Think it.
Magenta	Inspire it.
Red	Express it.
Red-Orange	Respect it.
Orange	Change it.
Gold	Play it.
Yellow	Know it.
Black	Feel it.
Brown	Realize it.
White	See it.

The aim of life is self-development. To realize one's nature perfectly—that is what each of us is here for. People are afraid of themselves, nowadays.

—OSCAR WILDE

Lime Green Power: Question It

Lime green gives you the stamina to question what is missing in your life. Ignite your passions by letting your inner voice speak. You will discover how you are yearning to feel. Questioning yourself gives you the power to know exactly what you need to do.

Exploring your thoughts is not the same as embracing them. Don't be afraid to confess your hidden, shocking considerations. They are simply clues to understanding yourself.

LIME GREEN AND YOU

The more you like lime green, the more you question what is missing in your life.

The less you like lime green, the more you avoid exploring what is missing in your life.

LOOK BEYOND YOUR SHOCKING THOUGHTS

Thoughts such as, "I need a divorce," "No one loves me," or "I am lazy," are not necessarily how you really feel. Look beyond them and consider your inner needs. Learning what makes you passionate will fire up your engine.

Everything starts—and ends—with you. You can travel around the world, moving from one city to another, but no matter where you go, you will create the same world again. Knowing your desires creates assertive, positive energy. Others will see you as exciting—they will feel that they know you, even when they first meet you.

SWEEP OUT THE COBWEBS

Complete every thought before you move to the next. If you don't, you will become scattered. Think about how it would feel if you actually did what you are thinking. Now think again. Do you really need to act on this thought? Make your mind razor sharp. Follow each thought or inner monologue to its conclusion.

Green Power: Be It

Green gives you a stronger understanding of yourself. Be true to the child in you by taking the time to make sure the "me" in you is okay. You will obtain the power of inner strength, able to create a more nurturing, supportive world.

Visit with this very real you by forgetting, for the moment, your immediate wants and others'. Only you will exist. You will be able to listen for what makes you or others comfortable. Your greater awareness will give you the power to be yourself or detect what others really need to be themselves.

GREEN AND YOU

The more you like green, the more aware you are of the support that you and others need.

The less you like green, the more unaware you are about what you and others need to be supported.

FIND A REFUGE

Find a park, beach, a special room, or a quiet café where you can monitor the conversation you are having with yourself. What do you really want? Be specific. What are you getting? Losing? Don't hold back. Bring all your forbidden wants to the surface. Repressing them is a waste of your time and energy.

Get to know the "I" within you. Make every thought start with *I*. Consider this *I* thought: "I am helping my friend because I want her to succeed," instead of, "She is in trouble so I have to help her." You are doing, for the most part, what you want to do. Own it, and you will see the contributions you are giving to the world.

BE RESPONSIBLE

Making your life just about you can be very exciting—and frightening. All of a sudden you are responsible for just yourself. If your feeling of being needed makes it difficult to be at peace with such a selfish thought, look deeper. Talk to yourself as if you were a small child. You will become comfortable visiting with just you.

Everyone is happier when you tell them what you want. Don't be so polite. Many times it is only a mechanism to avoid confronting your feelings or a situation. Tell yourself exactly what you want out of life.

BECOME A GREAT LISTENER

Allow your thoughts to be just about the other person. You will gain the power to listen for what gives voice to who they are before you consider yourself. Giving other people your full attention is a great compliment. You will make them feel comfortable—able to be themselves. Oops! All of a sudden you will also see who they really need to be.

CONSIDER YOUR FAVORITE COLOR

Now write down your favorite color and list three adjectives that describe why you like it.

Favorite Color	Adjectives
_____	1. _____
	2. _____
	3. _____

Doesn't this describe what you need to be yourself? Now look around. Where are you getting it? Not getting it?

Teal Power: Believe It

Teal inspires you to believe in your aspirations. Get intense. Wish over and over until you believe in your capacity to accomplish your dreams. Believe in your wish and you will gain the power to believe in yourself.

Don't judge yourself by who you are now. You are also who you dream to be! Ask others about their dreams. Now close your eyes, and visualize your own dream. Become inspired.

TEAL AND YOU

The more you like teal, the more you can appreciate your progress in attaining your dreams.

The less you like teal, the more difficult it is for you to feel that you are capable of achieving your dreams.

TALK UP YOUR DAY

What you tell yourself is very powerful. Ask yourself when you awake, "What makes me passionate?" After breakfast, "What can I do, or not do, today?" At the day's end, "What great things did I do today?"

Consistently acknowledge what you are accomplishing and you can even flip a negative situation into a positive, constructive adventure. Believe in your capabilities, and nothing will be able to slow you down.

DANCE EVERY DAY

When you listen to a song, you hear the melody and then the words. Let your passion for doing what you want to do be the melody in your life. Tune in to yourself and even your slowest songs will develop a distinctive upbeat tempo. After a while, you'll be dancing.

Protect the rhythm in your spirit. It will allow you to appreciate what you accomplish. Ask yourself, "Who am I?" Write down your thoughts. Constantly proclaim them every morning when you arise. You will become a believer in yourself—better able to accomplish your dream.

WHO DO YOU ASPIRE TO BE?

Name the person you most admire. Now list three adjectives that reflect why you admire this person. Record your responses below.

Person You Admire	Adjectives
_____	1. _____
	2. _____
	3. _____

Isn't this also who you aspire to be? If not, look again. Are you trying to please someone else more than yourself? Stop pretending. Make your own wish.

Blue Power: Dream It

Blue gives you the focus to visualize. Expand your mind by concentrating on your future. Dream. You will gain the power of mental discipline and be able to envision a more beautiful life.

Make a definite goal. Regularly assessing your future will keep you on the right road. Focus, focus, focus. Do not relent until you become your aspiration. Others will see your courage as self-confidence and want to be on your team.

BLUE AND YOU

The more you like blue, the more optimistic you are that your dreams will work.

The less you like blue, the more pessimistic you are that your dreams will work.

TAKE THE ULTIMATE RISK

Don't be shy. Say that you will do what you dream. Remember a time in your life when you really pushed yourself to go beyond what you believed you could do? Wasn't it exciting? Create this energized feeling again. Say you will make your dream a reality. The anticipation of that achievement will inspire you. Your life will have a sense of magic.

Take your dreams to the next level. Don't be influenced by a distracting situation or desires that undermine your willpower. Make your own course. Stay on your diet, cut down on or stop smoking, and don't call back the jerk that you miss.

BE CONCLUSIVE

Progress toward realizing your vision by eliminating the clutter of too many friends, expectations, or circumstances that demand your attention. They will drain your mental energy. Do one thing at a time. Take command of your future. Finish each goal.

FEEL YOUR FUTURE

Today's dreams are tomorrow's actions. Be aware of your feelings and thoughts. When you feel uncomfortable, chances are something is not working. Be less concerned with the answers than with the questions that need to be asked. Let them be your guide to success. Don't hesitate. Remember, no commitment equals no decision.

Completing statements such as "My objective is . . ." will keep you on track. You will see the important details. Be flexible. Examine first how a suggestion is like yours before you determine how it is different. This open-mindedness will make you smart—able to get the job done well and in less time.

PROCLAIM ALL YOUR DREAMS

Say all your dreams. Spell them out by filling in the blanks below.

Career:
In five years I will be _____

_____.

In ten years I will be _____

_____.

Relationships:

I will surround myself with _____.

(List those you respect and who respect you.)

Spiritual: I will be more true to myself by respecting my ability to

be _____, and _____, _____.

(List your strongest qualities.)

Indigo Power: Plan It

Indigo gives you enlightened perspectives to create successful plans. Dive into each ingredient you might need to realize your idea. You will gain the power to create an orchestrated, exciting future.

Establish an unrelenting focus by zeroing in on exactly how you can accomplish your goal, not on whether you can reach it. Dedicate your thoughts to clarifying why you need to do each thing in your plan, and you will be able to adopt a better or easier way of working—a shortcut to your dream.

INDIGO AND YOU

The more you like indigo, the more you believe in your ability to conceptualize new ideas.

The less you like indigo, the harder it is to believe that you need to make a plan.

BE ON THE BALL

Stay ahead of your deadlines by paying your bills on time, deciding in advance what you will cook for dinner, or with whom you will spend your time. Take charge of your life, or it will take charge of you. Plan ahead. You will gain the opportunity to create the future that you desire.

Get out a calendar. Write down what you will do each day to improve your relationships, have fun, or increase the size of your bank account. Sacrificing your time today will create a successful tomorrow. Invest in yourself. You can acquire wealth, perhaps a lovely home, or even a better love life.

PLAN A NEW YOU

Create a vision of your future. List three goals you want to achieve this year.

1. _____
2. _____
3. _____

Now, make a plan for achieving each one. For example:

My Goals	My Plans
1. A fun career	Focus on finding a new job
2. A deeper inner peace	Care more about others
3. More money	Spend less and invest

1. _____
2. _____
3. _____

The secret to staying focused is to get excited about your plan, not the goal. Assume you can do it, and your concerns will shift. They will become more conclusive. Others' opinions and current dilemmas will bother you less.

Purple Power: Think It

Purple creates the ability to see new possibilities, ideas, and strategies for yourself and others. Visit with your emotions. In them you will discover a greatness that once could only be imagined. You will gain the personal power to create something original.

Fight for what you believe. Don't be in a rush. Imagine that you have five years to accomplish your goals. Now what are the possibilities? Get emotional. Address your limitations beforehand so that you'll have no reservations about what you need to do. Once you've done this, go ahead full force, with all your heart. Manifesting your aspirations will make your dreams happen, no matter what.

PURPLE AND YOU

The more you like purple, the more prone you are to contemplation and self-examination.

The less you like purple, the more likely you are to deny your capabilities.

BE TRUE TO YOURSELF

Allow time for silence. Create a quiet space to hear the inner voices in your head. No, you are not crazy, and those voices are not aliens trying to direct your life. They are your emotions. Pay attention to the subtext of what they are saying.

Tune in to hearing the excitement in your own voice. It will reveal what you really love to do—which, of course, is what you will do best. Now look around you. Imagine who else you can be. Be courageous. Consider all your possibilities. Let your heart, not your head, speak. You will awaken the giant within you.

Deal from the top of the deck by bringing all the issues to the table. Examine your motivations. Now look at the other person's perspective or what the situation dictates. Only then can you reach a compromise. Stay motivated. Talk about what you think, and get others to do the same.

Failure occurs only when you give up. Even a definite *no* can later be a *yes*. When you are rejected or can't get what you want, consider why you really wanted it. Now look around. Where else can you get it? Keep looking until you find the same or a better way of reaching your objective. Never give up, and you will never fail.

Magenta Power: Inspire It

Magenta inspires you to start something new enthusiastically. When you are open to the world, your world will be open to you. Your pioneering spirit will help you gain the power to attract a new opportunity.

Create a spark. Start by discarding your skeptical thoughts. Focus instead on how exciting a person or place could be. Allow your curiosity and the quest for something entirely new to rule the moment. Your dynamic new body language will positively attract whatever you desire.

MAGENTA AND YOU

The more you like magenta, the more you are inspired by your environment.

The less you like magenta, the more suspicious you are of new things.

SMILE

A smile is inspiring. It creates exciting new situations. Remembering the fun you had in past endeavors can jump-start your day. Simply allow your natural curiosity to surface about something new. Others will feel it. Your feelings will attract the adventure you are seeking.

Make each day exciting. Let the world entertain you, but don't go overboard. Make sure that what you feel at the moment is what you desire in the long term. Enthusiasm is powerful. It can even spur you on to start things that you never intended doing.

HOW OFTEN DO YOU START THINGS?

Get a mirror, and put it next to your telephone.

Look at your expressions when you talk.

Are you smiling all the time? Oops! Things just seem to happen!

Are you never smiling? Lighten up! Don't be so suspicious.

BIG SMILES WIN

Your body language is actually more powerful than what you say. For fun, play this game with a friend. Look at him and say with a big smile on your face, "You are a jerk." If you are giving him a really big smile, he will smile back!

If you are having a bad time at a party, it's usually all about you. Walk into the bathroom or away from the crowd. Discard your negative, all-about-me thoughts. Now, practice smiling and return. Look around. Become curious

about someone. Give him a big smile from your heart, and
the fun will begin.

Red Power: Express It

Red gives you the practical knowledge and expressive power
to direct your life. Speak up. Tell the world who you are and
what you want. You will gain the power to make your life
and things around you work.

Be specific. Let others know what they can expect from
you and what you are expecting from them. Tell them about
your strengths and weaknesses and in what areas you need
help to be successful. Tell your boss that you can do your job,
and tell your partner what you need to be happier. Your world
will become more about what you require to be a success.

RED AND YOU

The more you like red, the less tolerance you have for
failure or incompetence.

The less you like red, the more you will tolerate things
that you do not enjoy.

BE SPECIFIC

Get control of your environment, or it will control you.
What are you doing right now? Exactly what do you need
to do? Get out your magnifying glass. Look at each thought
and activity that is absorbing your time. Direct your energy
toward people and situations that are worth your attention.
Others will feel your energy. They will know you are not
playing games.

Tell others specifically what you can or can't do. You will become able to produce what they expect—a success. If you are not being direct and specific, or if they are stubbornly focused on themselves, they can perceive "facts" about you that are false.

SAY IT . . . POWERFULLY!

Over the course of my twenty-four years in the personnel field, I met many human-resources executives who had the capability to be president or CEO of their companies. Yet they did not get promoted. Their low-key self-presentation was perceived as not being powerful.

Expressing who you are, whether in a personal or professional situation, allows others to know what you can do. If you don't tell them who you are, don't expect them to know. Like it or not, you are going to be perceived as who you say you are. Oops! Ultimately, how you are perceived by others is how you perceive yourself, right? Turn up the volume. Make strong, definite statements.

Red-Orange Power: Respect It

Red-orange gives you the self-respect to honor your individuality. Respecting yourself starts with appreciating those around you. Honor those who love and respect you, and you will gain the power to honor yourself.

Make time for whoever or whatever is important to you. Your focused efforts will get things done and show others how much you care. Consider the people and issues you think about. Aren't they the most important in your life? If not, get your act together.

RED-ORANGE AND YOU

The more you like red-orange, the more you honor your individuality.

The less you like red-orange, the more difficult it is for you to distinguish yourself from society.

MAKE TIME FOR WHAT IS IMPORTANT

I have had the same housekeeper for more than twenty-five years. She is really famous among my friends for her fried chicken. One day when I asked how she made such incredibly delicious chicken, she replied, "I just know when to take it off the fire." She cared enough to devote her time to watching the fire.

Little children know the importance of time. They know instinctively, the moment they see you, how much you care about them. Take the time to feel each person's heart. Investing your time to connect with the humanity inside of each person will not reward you every time, but overall you will get back much more love than you gave out.

RESPECT YOURSELF

Ask yourself, *Do those I listen to listen to me? Do those I love, love me?* When you give to people by thinking of their needs or by being with them, you give them your most valuable gift—your time. You make them important to you. Are they making you important to them as well? If not, why continue? Direct your emotions and your time toward those who have authentic concern and love for you.

LET YOUR HEART LEAD

So who would you miss? Pretend that the world is coming to an end and that you can save only your family and five other people you care about. Consider who they are.

Now, write or tell each of them why you care about him or her. His or her sincere appreciation will make you feel worthwhile. Your spirit will bask in the ultimate sunshine—love.

Orange Power: Change It

Orange makes positive change easier for you. It enables you to disassociate from what you expect from yourself to realize the clarity of a situation. You gain the power to eliminate or change the direction of dead-end situations and relationships.

Be realistic about what you promise or expect. Everyone is happier when you're realistic about what you can and can't do. How long will it take you to finish? Is there enough time? Reevaluate your expectations of yourself and others frequently. When you find yourself working harder or feeling too serious, ask those around you, "How am I doing?"

ORANGE AND YOU

The more you like orange, the easier it is for you to disassociate from your expectations to see the truth of a situation.

The less you like orange, the more you tend to expect from yourself—more than you can deliver.

DO WHAT YOU SAY

I overheard a friend in Atlanta telling her aunt that she could be in West Virginia by seven o'clock, in time for dinner. When I asked, "How can you drive from Atlanta to West Virginia in eight hours?" she said defensively, "I drive really fast." I insisted we look at the mileage.

We computed that if she drove 120 miles per hour, never stopping to eat or get gas, she would arrive at four o'clock the next morning. She was about to let her aunt down and fail, no matter how well she performed.

UNDER-PROMISE, OVER-DELIVER

Instead of working harder and harder to make a situation or a relationship work, simply ask the folks around you, "How am I doing?" If you are sincere, they will tell you. A word of caution: If someone says, "Everything is fine," and looks uncomfortable, ask the same question again.

Acknowledge how long it will take to accomplish each thing that you are going to do before you promise to do it. Everyone will be happier, including you, when you tell them what you can and can't do up front. Ha! Why not be marvelous? Promise less than what you believe you can deliver. Okay, now breathe.

Gold Power: Play It

Gold gives you the power to rediscover what gives you pleasure. Ignite your inner fire. Give yourself time to do what feels good. Play. Your new awareness of exciting people and situations will give you the power to dismiss and eventually discard your undesirable thoughts and get out of negative situations.

Your new, carefree, more passionate perspective will convey confidence and attract friends and business. Always doing what you are supposed to be doing will run your battery down. Do what your heart desires, and your energy will zoom.

GOLD AND YOU

The more you like gold, the more you know how to use your resources to create new things.

The less you like gold, the more your undesirable thoughts distract you from knowing what makes you passionate.

PLAY KEEPS YOU ON TRACK

Listen to the tone of other people's voices. It is easy to hear who is full of passion and who has lost it. Don't become a zombie. If you are constantly doing what you are supposed to do, not what you enjoy, you will lose your spirit as well.

Keep your passions on track by having fun each day. Create the downtime to feel your essence. Only then will you know how you really feel. You will see what makes you passionate and be able to eliminate your undesirable thoughts. Say yes, not no, to the adventure of being alive.

THE PLAY GAME

"Unplan" your day off. In the example below, your day off is Saturday. So, let's begin with the night before.

Friday night, after 9:00 P.M., discard your thoughts about work and stop watching TV or doing any serious reading. Turn off your phone and your alarm. Before you go to bed, let your thoughts roam free.

Saturday, when you awake, think, *What do I want to do today?* Don't rush. Allow time for just *you*. Take a bath, shower, or go for a walk. Keep it quiet. Avoid playing music or listening to the radio.

You will start to experience a deeper awareness of your desires. Respect these feelings as the source of all your passion.

Yellow Power: Know It

Yellow gives you the wisdom to know what you need. Critique the ongoing conversation you are having with yourself by reevaluating what you are getting from people and situations. You will gain the power to know what motivates you and see the reality of others.

Seek the reality of each situation or what each person is motivated to accomplish. Don't waste your time on something you cannot change or someone who doesn't know what he wants. Each person or situation is in a particular state for a reason. Accept that, and move on to what fits your sensibility or to the people who will support you the most.

YELLOW AND YOU

The more you like yellow, the more willing you are to get information before coming to conclusions.

The less you like yellow, the sooner you come to a conclusion, even if you have not heard all the facts.

EVERYONE IS DOING THEIR OWN THING

Accept the fact that your thoughts are just about you. Even when you are helping someone, you are doing your own thing. Your contribution is making you feel worthwhile. Pay attention. What are you getting from what you do? Determine what others are getting as well.

Look to your own motivation. If one moment you are intensely concerned with yourself, and the next, overly concerned with other people and their business, beware. Confess the reason you are doing what you are doing. You will gain the inner peace of knowing the power and limitations of each relationship or circumstance.

LET THE SUN SHINE

Your spirit knows only the moment. A period of gloom can appear to last forever. Accept that gloom is a frame of mind in which you try to understand yourself, and a sunny mood is a good facilitator of self-expression. Together, they make up the process of being human. You need both.

For fun on a rainy day, pretend that it is bright and sunny. You will draw others to you like crazy. Your high energy will give them the hope to start looking beyond the gloom of the day. After all, a positive thought is the beginning of a new tomorrow.

Black Power: Feel It

Black gives you the courage to know your emotions. Take the plunge. Feel both your pleasant and painful experiences, but don't obsess over them. You will experience the power of genuine appreciation for yourself and others.

Not recognizing what you feel controls your emotions and, eventually, your actions. Thoughts such as *Everything about that person [or situation] is perfect* or *Is life worth living?* are warning signs that you are avoiding a self-truth. Ask friends for their input. Take notes and think hard about their comments every morning when you arise. This practice will help you give your life more value.

BLACK AND YOU

The more you like black, the more you are ruled by your emotions.

The less you like black, the more you avoid your emotions.

BE FIRST-CLASS

Give each person you meet a part of you. They will, for the most part, become more in tune with their humanity. To hide your heart and not relate on a personal level is to be forgotten the minute you leave the room. Look each person in the eye. Say hello with your heart, and good-bye using the person's name. Be first-class; show the world you have style.

Treasure those around you, and they will respect you. Always appreciate their contributions. Be sincere. Watch your pronouns. *We* creates a union: *I* is all about you. Isn't class simply honoring the humanity within each person?

YOUR UPS AND DOWNS

You and everyone else exist in a constant flux of mood swings. Your darker side (your emotions) allows you to feel what you need. Your lighter side (your thoughts) gives you the ability to distinguish whom or what you want.

Be serious about your life, not yourself. Trust your emotions, and surrender your ego. Otherwise, your emotions or frustrations will begin to build. Then you will react. The longer you wait, the more dramatic your reaction will be. Give equal respect to both the light and dark sides of yourself.

> The dark is equally important as the light.
> —CHARLOTTE BRONTË

Brown Power: Realize It

Brown grounds you. Immerse yourself in understanding the natural process of life. Get to really know a person or situation before you judge it. You will gain the power of awareness, becoming able to embrace life, people, and things as they are.

Be real. Don't get caught up in the rat race or try to gain everyone's approval. Forget about power and status. The more airs you put on and the harder you try to disguise your shortcomings, the more apparent they are for everyone to see. You'll make stronger connections with others by accepting yourself as you are.

BROWN AND YOU

The more you like brown, the more aware you are of your environment and the temporary nature of life.

The less you like brown, the longer it takes you to recognize the realities of your environment and life itself.

LIFE'S GREATEST LESSON

Farmers, the old-fashioned types without fancy equipment or irrigation systems, are very grounded. They live a life in which a crop planting can be ruined because of lack of rain. Imagine working very hard for months, doing everything right, and coming up with nothing.

Accepting failure, without taking it personally, is life's greatest lesson. People and things just are. Are you grounded in reality? Pay attention to your thoughts. Accept the benefits of your failures. Many uncomfortable situations or relationships teach you great lessons.

THE UNIVERSE IS TALKING TO YOU

Every time you start a project without honestly appraising the situation or yourself, you are setting yourself up for a fall. Below are a few arrogant behaviors that will come back to haunt you.

Arrogance #1	Arrogance #2	Arrogance #3
"I'm really attractive" So . . . your need to prove yourself makes you artificial, unattractive.	"I'm better than everyone" So . . . others see you as a conceited jerk, not of importance to them.	"I know everything" So . . . you don't listen and know very little.

> Pride goeth before destruction, and a
> haughty spirit before a fall.
> —PROVERBS 16:1

White Power: See It

White gives you the objectivity to see all of your available options. Step back and view your world as if you were not a part of it. Let your sharp eye roam into every facet of your life. In keeping your distance, you will gain the power to decipher new opportunities for yourself and those you love.

Being objective allows you to determine the possible resources available. Ponder this question: In the entire world, if you could have anything, what or who would it be? Now look at your current relationships and circumstances and decide what you need to change, request, keep, or let go.

WHITE AND YOU

The more you like white, the faster you are able to shift gears and explore new options.

The less you like white, the longer it takes you to break free of problematic situations.

DISTANCE CREATES OBJECTIVITY

When you get upset or feel uncomfortable, think about the price you are paying for what you want. Take a step back. Be objective. Making your life complicated has more to do with your mind-set than your environment.

Distance gives clarity. It gives you the control to regain yourself.

YOUR VICES AND VIRTUES

Your greatest talents and your greatest weaknesses are the same. If you attack your weaknesses, you stand the risk of losing your greatness.

> Every vice is only an exaggeration of a necessary and virtuous function.
> —RALPH WALDO EMERSON

With time, however, and an investigative spirit, you can focus on where your virtues end and your vices begin. Being completely objective with yourself will allow you to cut away your negative qualities without sacrificing your positive ones.

Vice/Virtue #1	Vice/Virtue #2	Vice/Virtue #3
You can be close-minded to other people's views, so you possess a persistent focus.	You finish tasks without knowing all the facts, so you make decisions on time.	You expend a lot of energy on unnecessary things, so you eliminate failure before it occurs.

BE TRUE TO YOURSELF

Keep the power within you by staying aware of the "don'ts." Avoid letting the obstacles mentioned below stop you from realizing your self or your place in the world. Be true to yourself and respect others by acknowledging their right to claim their own authenticity.

Don't Force Change

If you feel that you are in a rush to change, you are not accepting yourself, someone else, or a situation as it already exists. Change begins with awareness. It gives you the power to better direct and manage your actions.

Don't Generalize

Generalizations are usually inaccurate. When you use words such as *always* or *never,* be careful. You will lose the ability to see facts. Open up your life to the world around you. Opportunity can exist only if you allow it to.

Don't Disagree at the Start

When someone disagrees with you, make an effort to see his or her point of view. Many times you are both right. Use the word *and* more. For example, consider that you could do this and he could do that, or you can be this way and she can be that way. Accept that whatever the other person says is okay. Then think about it again. This is a good way to see if your point of disagreement is important enough to argue about.

Don't Lightly Dismiss Your Defensiveness

Whenever you say, "I do not deserve that" or "I did not do that," you are being defensive. Aren't you just uncomfortable with something about yourself? Stop pushing so hard, and the facts will surface. You will be able to focus on what you want. Then tell others what they can expect from you.

Don't Make Assumptions

Other people's feelings are not always about you. Are they sad, nervous, or confident? Ask; don't assume. Try to get more information. If you think you know what others are going to say or exactly how a situation will develop, you are not keeping an open mind.

Don't Surround Yourself with People Who Do Not Believe in or Respect You

Real friends listen to how you feel and even question what you do. When friends fail to point out when you've stepped out of line, they are doing you a disservice. A true friend will ground you in reality.

Don't Beat Yourself Up

When you talk down to yourself, little by little you destroy your passion. Emotions should be nurtured, not torn down. To say, "I am . . . [fat, old, ugly, stupid, dizzy, crazy, etc.]" is destructive. Don't have unrealistic expectations. Give yourself the room to accomplish what you're capable of. You will become a winner.

Don't Try to Make Your Emotions More Logical

Your feelings are distinct from your thought processes. Respect your emotions by never questioning them. By separating your heart from your mind, you give both the freedom to breathe. You will actually gain more control. Humor your emotions or you will lose yourself.

Don't Say Never

When you say, "I will never love, be hurt, or express that again," you destroy a part of you. You lose a perspective you need and undermine possibilities for your future. When you feel empty or become uncomfortable, be careful. Learn to forgive and forget.

BE YOURSELF

> To give up your individuality is to annihilate yourself.
> —ROBERT INGERSOLL

You were born innocent. This childlike quality in you *is* you. Whenever you put up walls, you lose your pure, passionate spirit. Accept your feelings about the world around you, or you will lose sight of your real self. Make your life a passionate journey by trusting your inner voice. Take the Dewey Color System Oath:

> I will honor my self-truth by doing what I most enjoy and will respect others by accepting their right to go the way they want to go.

Remember when you were a child and you thought you could fly? Well, you were right. Trust your inner self by being yourself. Respect others by allowing for their need to be who they are. Awareness will be your trophy. Your spirit will soar.

Trust Your Intuition

How do you feel right after you walk away from a person or situation? Spend a moment listening to yourself. Are you content, exhilarated, angry, or even depressed? Listen to your inner voice. It consistently tells you what will bode well for your future.

Surround yourself with exciting people and situations. Their positive energy will give you the strength to stand back and reject what does not work. Admiration is energizing, and disgust is debilitating.

Be devoted to respecting the positive people and situations in your life. After a while, you will simply discard the negative. Choose the sunny side, and your passions will flourish. You will be able to accomplish anything you desire.

On a Final Note

Life is like a roller-coaster ride. Appreciate your dark, twisting tunnels—your emotions. You'll clarify why you feel how you feel or do what you do, and this new you will become empowered to "turn on the lights" and really enjoy the joyful, thrilling experience of life.

My hope is that by reading *The Dewey Color System* you have illuminated the passion and power within you, and that you now know how to give more support to those you love.

Your life is precious. Honor your inner passion and your spirit by committing yourself to creating a life in which you can fully be yourself at home, at work, or wherever you go!

ADDITIONAL COLOR PAGES

MY COLOR CATEGORY PAGE

Name: _____

Your color category selections:

CATEGORY	FAVORITE	LEAST FAVORITE
Primary		
Secondary		
Achromatic		
Intermediate		

MY COLOR CATEGORY PAGE

Name: _____

Your color category selections:

CATEGORY	FAVORITE	LEAST FAVORITE
Primary		
Secondary		
Achromatic		
Intermediate		

MY COLOR CATEGORY PAGE

Name: _____

Your color category selections:

CATEGORY	FAVORITE	LEAST FAVORITE
Primary		
Secondary		
Achromatic		
Intermediate		

MY COLOR CATEGORY PAGE

Name: _____

Your color category selections:

CATEGORY	FAVORITE	LEAST FAVORITE
Primary		
Secondary		
Achromatic		
Intermediate		

MY COLOR CATEGORY PAGE

Name: _____

Your color category selections:

CATEGORY	FAVORITE	LEAST FAVORITE
Primary		
Secondary		
Achromatic		
Intermediate		

RESOURCES

Color Products Available from Energia Press®

THE DEWEY COLOR COORDINATOR $28.00

Take this book with you when you're buying clothes or furnishings. At a glance you will see seventy-six colors that coordinate with your attire, furniture, or walls. Use this brilliant shopping guide to make your world more spiritual, sensual, and adventurous.

DEWEY COLOR KIDS $8.95

Give your child the gift of passionate, brilliant color. This interactive children's book for ages six months to eight years old will teach your child basic color and reading skills. Use it in conjunction with *The Dewey Color System* to better understand how to be supportive without destroying your child's essence.

DEWEY COLOR CARDS $18.95

Inspire new perspectives with brilliant color in this array of fifteen magnificently printed greeting cards that share the powerful vibrations of color. Each card has a vellum envelope and an inspirational message. There is plaenty of room to write your own message too.

DEWEY COLOR PUZZLE $8.99

Put your color skills to the test. This fun, fast puzzle will challenge your ability to see color. Complete it in less than five minutes, and you are a chromatic expert. Practice makes perfect. Do it over and over to sharpen your visual color skills.

DEWEY COLOR CHAMELEONS $15.95

The Dewey Color Chameleon sports fifteen power-color shirts, and you will want to collect them all! Each color has its own meaning.

For the store nearest you, call 1-866-351-5001 or log on to our website www.deweycolorsystem.com.

Check Out Our Website

Visit www.deweycolorsystem.com and obtain digital passion profiles. You can select personal printouts for yourself, or e-mail your friends and loved ones with a printout gift. Below is a sample profile list.

YOUR COLOR TYPE: MORE PEACE, MORE HAPPINESS

Gain powerful insights into how you see yourself and how others see you in your relationships and career.

HUE ARE YOU: MORE INSIGHT, MORE PASSION

By focusing on yourself, you will solve problems easily, make successful decisions, and approach the world with power.

RELATIONSHIPS: MORE LOVE, MORE SEX

Learn how you function in your relationships and create strong bonds with those you love. Invite someone special to join you.

CAREER: MORE MONEY, MORE FUN

Determine how to prioritize the rewarding areas of your life while maintaining your steam and vigor. Obstacles will become insignificant details.

FULL PERSONAL EVALUATION

This fourteen-page proven evaluation explains *you* in compelling detail, with astounding accuracy.

FULL COMPATIBILITY EVALUATION

This sixteen-page customized evaluation explains the contributions of your partner and the supportive nature of your relationship in amazing detail.

Order a profile, a copy of *The Dewey Color System*, and much more directly from our website, or write to: Energia®, Inc., P.O. Box 669306, Marietta, Georgia 30066.

ACKNOWLEDGMENTS

Louise Moses Sadka, my mom, for teaching me how to think.

Dewey Sadka Sr., my dad, for his unrelenting faith in my ability.

Jennifer Burris, my apprentice and vice president of product development, for ten years of complete devotion to making my color theory a reality.

Roberto Athayde, for exposing me to a world that inspired my creation.

Mary Ann Petro, for her brilliant, knowledgeable perspectives of color and design.

Queenie Sadka Nassour, for showing me the power of passionate love.

Lillie Mae Sams, for twenty-five years of love and concern.

Ellis Nassour, for his editing insights and for keeping this project on track.